THE AUSTIN-SAN ANTONIO MEGAREGION

THE TEXAS EXPERIENCE

*Books made possible by
Sarah '84 and Mark '77 Philpy*

The Austin– San Antonio Megaregion

OPPORTUNITY AND CHALLENGE IN THE LONE STAR STATE

Henry Cisneros, Robert Rivard, and David Hendricks

Texas A&M University Press
College Station

(∞) This paper meets the requirements of ANSI/NISO
Z39.48-1992 (Permanence of Paper).
Binding materials have been chosen for durability.

Library of Congress Control Number: 2025938960
Identifiers: LCCN: 2025938960 | ISBN 9781648433382 (cloth) |
ISBN 9781648433399 (ebook)
LC record available at https://lccn.loc.gov/2025938960

CONTENTS

PREFACE

This book began as an effort to highlight the sheer magnitude of growth in Central Texas driven by the dynamism of the two anchor cities—Austin and San Antonio—and rapid expansion over the last decade of residences, commercial businesses, and industries in the dozens of contiguous communities that make the region a rapidly expanding network of economic and social activity. One report after another has chronicled unprecedented growth in every measurable category—population, job growth and employment, new business starts, manufacturing indices, traffic counts, in-migration, school attendance, and airport enplanements. These census and economic reports reflect record-breaking growth compared to historic levels and document the Austin–San Antonio metro areas as the fastest-growing region in the nation. At various points over the last several years, Austin has been the top-ranked major city in the nation by percentage of population growth, while San Antonio has been third. San Antonio in absolute growth gained more population within its city limits in 2023 than any other US city, adding 21,970 new residents, the equivalent of 60 newcomers, some of them newborns, arriving every day to make the city their home. San Antonio also had the most numeric growth in the nation in 2017 and 2021. In 2022, Georgetown, north of Austin on the I-35 corridor, was the nation's fastest-growing city, with more than fifty thousand population, while the cities of Kyle, Leander, and New Braunfels ranked in the top fifteen. Comal and Hays Counties have each been the fastest-growing counties in the nation in their respective size categories.

It was our initial intent to simply document these trends in a cogent way and present a regional reality that is not yet verifiably evident to many residents of the region or widely recognized nationally. It seemed to be important to paint a coherent picture of two adjoining metropolitan areas that are coalescing into a single megaregion, one that surpassed 5 million people in 2023 and will grow to 8.3 million people by 2050, only twenty-five years from now. In the course of writing the narrative of this demonstrable growth, it became clear that there is much more to the story. We were led to a second stream of thinking, a second rationale, for writing this book. The simple question "So what?" prompted a deeper examination of the significance and impact of this growth. The answers came tumbling forth. State, regional, and local leaders need to rethink transportation systems to handle new traffic loads of all kinds: surface traffic on roadways, mass transit connections across the region, and world-class air connectivity. The production of more housing of all types—single-family and multifamily residences, inner-city and new suburban units, affordable and upscale housing, and shelter for the completely unhoused—has fallen woefully behind the demand created by such rapid population growth. That, in turn, has led to rising costs for both homeowners and renters competing for scarce inventory. Education and training programs must be strengthened across the region to meet the workforce requirements of new technology and advanced manufacturing firms and to ensure reliable paths of upward mobility for all populations across the region. Prosperity for some while leaving behind significant subpopulations will not be a good outcome. The pace of new growth must be supported by basic infrastructure improvements to water supply, energy and power, environmental safeguards, and climate change mitigation and by quality-of-life amenities such as the preservation and expansion of precious open spaces. These are the prerequisites for sustaining the economic attractiveness and quality attributes that have heretofore created this moment of unprecedented growth. The challenge of addressing these needs generates questions such as, Is so much growth good for the region, and if it is, are we prepared for it?

These questions necessarily take us into a philosophical realm that drives the third motivation for this book. We realized that it is no longer a question of whether Austin–San Antonio leaders and residents want this growth. The region has emerged as a hot spot in the nation, creating both opportunity and challenge. It is, of course, easier to take advantage of the opportunities and much more difficult to meet the challenges.

There are many reasons why economic leaders around the country and beyond see this region as such an attractive destination to do business, grow, and prosper. Texas offers abundant land for commercial and residential development; a growing educated populace; five of the most dynamic, fastest-growing metros in the country; business-friendly tax policies; and a welcoming state government. Texas personifies opportunity for many, be they frustrated California tech leaders or graduating university students looking for good jobs and a sustainable, affordable lifestyle.

This opportunity-challenge dynamic led us to a different logic. Essentially, the case is this: If it is inevitable that we will grow at globally significant rates, then we clearly have to plan smartly for it. The swing between failing to prepare and successfully preparing is vast. If we fail to prepare, we choose to live with gridlock and congestion, environmental damage, social contentiousness, inadequate utility services, and perpetuated inequities. One might say that this is a path for squandering the upside promises that growth can create. On the other hand, how many other major metro areas anticipate such record growth, in-migration, and opportunity? Why not capitalize on those competitive advantages by addressing and mitigating the attendant challenges?

We hope this book gives the state's top elected officials and the megaregion's local governmental entities—the city, county, and regional agencies—motivation and ideas for cooperation and unity in planning for the accommodation of continued record population and economic growth. We do not propose a model from another place that has faced similar challenges. Meeting the challenges in Texas in the coming decades will not be done by looking west to California, which is losing population and struggling with budget deficits despite its state income tax. Nor will working models be found in Florida or New York, the most populous states to the east. Texas is unique, with its own distinct history, cultures, and regional customs. Texans have always gone their own way, and a future path forward must be shaped by state and local leaders acting within the state's traditions.

If we do choose to act, this region can be the model of the American Dream in the first half of the twenty-first century: a place where the American system of enterprise and public-sector collaboration can result in productivity, innovation, inclusive opportunities, greater shared prosperity, and a higher standard of living. In reflecting on these stakes and on the urgency of this moment, the exhortative character of this book took form.

The task before us is not easy, but it can be done. It is not a matter of liberal or conservative politics, of red or blue ideologies; it is a matter of realistic leadership and practical public consensus. The reality of the Austin–San Antonio megaregion is becoming more evident every day to those of us who live here. We try in this book to undergird those impressions with facts, data, and scenarios for the future. Hopefully, enough of us in the general public will insist upon foresighted action from our leaders in all the sectors that touch our lives in the Austin–San Antonio megaregion.

ACKNOWLEDGMENTS

The coauthors wish to express their thanks to KLRN-TV in San Antonio for producing its 2023 documentary on the Austin–San Antonio region, which coincided with the development of this book. The KLRN team included president and CEO Arthur Emerson, director of news and production Shari St. Clair, cameraman Larry Burns, and video editor Christina Rodriguez-Romo. Their skills and insights helped inform this book. The one-hour documentary, *San Antonio–Austin: The Emerging Mega-Metro*, can be seen online at http://www.klrn.org.

The authors also wish to thank Texas Mutual and Barshop & Oles Co. for their financial support of both the documentary and the book.

The authors are grateful for the data work by the Texas Demographic Center at the downtown campus of the University of Texas at San Antonio. The center's work and the availability of its website supplied key findings for the book.

The authors thank all the business, civic, government, and sports leaders in the Austin–San Antonio region who gave their time and insights in interviews for both the book and the documentary.

The maps by Mike Fisher and photos supplied by Al Rendon also greatly enhanced this book.

We additionally thank the staff of Texas A&M University Press for its editing and production work on the book.

Support staff members for Henry Cisneros provided vital assistance too. They include Claudia Vasquez, Sylvia Arce, Lisa Martinez, Nora Clark, and Quiana Natividad.

Every word in the book was made possible ultimately by the backing of the authors' intelligent, patient, and enabling spouses. We express our love and gratitude to Mary Alice Cisneros, Monika Maeckle, and Lucila Chavez Hendricks.

THE AUSTIN–SAN ANTONIO MEGAREGION

The Inevitability of the Austin–San Antonio Megaregion

In my forty-plus years of living in Austin and San Antonio, I spent a lot of time on I-35, and I've seen the corridor develop. At this stage, I believe it is not only an inevitability that this becomes a megaregion; I believe it becomes a necessity that we do that work intentionally to the benefit of our communities. We are leaning in on the thoughtful planning that needs to be done now in collaboration with our partners along the I-35 corridor.

—Former San Antonio Mayor Ron Nirenberg

It's going to require us to pay twenty-first-century attention to this region. I think, if we do it right, it becomes a megaregion. It might become a megaregion organically, but we could do a whole lot with it.

—Austin Mayor Kirk Watson

For decades, the Austin–San Antonio conversation was about contrasts and competition: the self-proclaimed "Live Music Capital of the World" and emerging tech hub, home to state government and the flagship University of Texas (UT) campus, versus the Alamo City, with its Hispanic heritage, UNESCO World Heritage recognition of its Spanish colonial missions, deep

The Texas Triangle: The Austin–San Antonio metropolitan areas have merged to form a unified urban region that is one corner of the Texas Triangle. The Triangle comprises 35 of the state's 254 counties. The 35 counties are in Texas' four largest metropolitan statistical areas: Dallas–Fort Worth, Houston, Austin, and San Antonio. Map by Mike Fisher.

military roots, a growing biosciences and research sector, and a vibrant tourism economy. Located seventy-four miles away from each other on Interstate 35, the two fast-growing cities seemed to exist in different worlds, with a few relatively quiet suburban smaller cities along and around the corridor. There was still a lot of pastureland visible to travelers moving up and down the interstate.

San Antonio was bigger population-wise, but Austin's population was better educated, its city less defined in part by poverty and historic exclusion. It was more of a destination city for students choosing the university, young professionals seeking good jobs, and everyone drawn to the capital's laid-back lifestyle and culture. Competition rather than collaboration seemed to define the two cities' relationship, with many in San Antonio feeling their city compared unfavorably to Austin, a feeling readily confirmed by many Austinites.

Not anymore. The word *megaregion* has seemingly entered the vocabulary of every area officeholder, urban planner, and business leader deeply invested in the Austin–San Antonio corridor. Growth has erased the physical separation and joined the two cities like never before. Cow pastures are long gone along most of the interstate, replaced by growing midsized cities, the arrival of Amazon and other warehouse operations, the ever-growing San Marcos retail hub, and dense traffic all hours of the day.

"We are living in an unprecedented moment of opportunity in Texas, better than the opportunities found in any other state, opportunities to innovate, to start and grow businesses, to recruit and retain talent, and to work to make prosperity a reality for many more of the people who live in Austin and San Antonio and all the surrounding cities," said Graham Weston, chairman of Weston Ventures, which is engaged in major developments and redevelopments in San Antonio's downtown.

Speaking at the University of Texas at San Antonio's Alvarez College of Business as the annual Frost Distinguished Speaker in February 2023, Weston, the former cofounder and chairman of Rackspace, the cloud computing company, said more and more people are coming to the region every day because they know they will discover opportunities not found in other states.

"The trends are unstoppable," Weston told the hundreds of business students gathered for his talk.

Demographers all agree the growth is unstoppable. That's been evident for years now, but the pace of growth has outpaced earlier predictions. More than a decade ago, Austin Mayor Steve Adler and San Antonio Mayor Ivy Taylor both agreed in public remarks that the two metros or their corridor cities needed to learn how to work together rather than against each other as I-35 rivals. The cooperation back then was more rhetorical than real, but it signaled something significant, even if the changes were not measurable overnight. Austin and San Antonio realized their economic futures were intertwined and that once unimaginable opportunity could be glimpsed on the horizon if local leaders could see what the rest of the world was starting to see: The two big cities and all the growing midsized cities were becoming a single megaregion.

Dallas and Fort Worth had come to the same realization more than a half century earlier, leading to the 1974 opening of the Dallas / Fort Worth International Airport—DFW—three letters that soon became shorthand for the entire multicounty area once known as the Metroplex. The former state demographer and US Census Bureau Director Steve Murdock said Austin and San Antonio were not as closely linked geographically or demographically as Dallas and Fort Worth, separated only by thirty-two miles. Yet the Central Texas growth into a single urban-suburban colossus was inevitable, Murdock said. Coming generations would treat Austin–San Antonio as a single megaregion and would refer to the two major cities as a single entity even if each city remained culturally and economically distinct.

If anything, the demographic predictions for growth in the two metros and adjacent cities proved far too conservative, as Texas became the runaway number-one destination state for companies and individuals looking to leave states with fewer employment opportunities, state income taxes, and stricter regulatory state governments. A December 2023 report by CBRE, the global commercial research giant, identified Austin as the number-one destination for corporate relocations between 2018 and 2023, with 66 of the 209 relocations to Texas happening in Austin, more than double the 32 company relocations to Dallas and 25 to Houston. In contrast, San Francisco / San Jose led all cities with 79 company departures, followed by Los Angeles / Irvine with 50 and, on the East Coast, 21 that left New York City.

Many companies not ready to move corporate headquarters have chosen Texas for significant expansion. Texas' elected leaders are unabashedly probusiness and welcoming, and that message has proved attractive to a long list of corporations looking to expand in more favorable climates. Large corporations like Oracle and Tesla are among the more familiar Fortune 500 companies that moved corporate headquarters from California to Austin. (Oracle announced in 2024 it would move its headquarters again, to Nashville, Tennessee.) Google, Apple, and Facebook, all based on the West Coast, are major presences in Austin driving the city's rapid high-end job growth.

San Antonio, while not a destination for major corporate relocations, is enjoying its own economic development successes, most recently announcing the arrival of the British heavy-equipment manufacturer JCB, which will build its second major plant in North America on the city's South Side, employing 1,500 workers in advanced manufacturing jobs.

The rush to relocate to Texas seems unaffected by the state's increasingly conservative elected leaders and their controversial policies to militarize the Texas-Mexico border and target asylum seekers and other undocumented workers, as well as the state's harsh antiabortion laws and attacks on LGBTQ rights.

Fast-forward from a decade ago to the present, and here is what the data tell us about the Austin–San Antonio metro areas: The entire region, large and small cities, is growing at a faster rate than all other metro regions. The Austin–San Antonio metro areas continued to grow even in 2020 and 2021 during the COVID-19 pandemic. While civic and business leaders in both metros, as well as those in the corridor cities, embrace the megaregion concept with much greater commitment today, they also recognize the absence of a regional entity capable of addressing the looming challenges that come with record growth. It's a major concern for the region's mayors, business leaders, and urban planners.

Daily life in this urban Southwest destination is increasingly impacted, negatively, by these leading concerns: the lack of a mass transit option as gridlock grips the I-35 corridor, the continuing vulnerability of the state's energy grid, Austin's single water source dependency, acute infrastructure investment needed in the corridor cities, and extreme weather incidents attributed to climate change. The shortage of affordable housing grows worse by the quarter as hundreds of new residents to the region arrive daily while housing starts lagging badly behind. Both cities have growing populations of middle-class families who cannot afford to buy homes. The shortage of available homes for sale, housing experts say, is largely due to population growth that far outpaces new housing starts and has driven up the competition and pricing of available housing stock. One measure: More and more residential properties for sale attract winning bids above original asking prices. Rising home values coupled with inflation and high interest rates have shut out many first-time homebuyers.

Homelessness also is on the rise. San Antonio has the second-highest poverty rate of major cities in the state at 17.7 percent, notably higher than Austin's 12.4 percent. Both cities have significant populations of economically disadvantaged families whose monthly rent payments dangerously exceed the maximum recommended level of 30 percent of gross income. San Antonio housing authorities maintain a waiting list of more than one hundred thousand families awaiting subsidized housing.

"More than 90 percent of the families sending their forty-six thousand children to our schools are economically disadvantaged and one missed paycheck away from a crisis," said Dr. Jaime Aquino, superintendent of the San Antonio Independent School District, the largest inner-city public school district in the city. "The impact on the mental health and well-being of these families is often overlooked, but it is profound."

So can the Austin–San Antonio region continue to enjoy greater growth and prosperity even as its vulnerabilities grow in concert? Clearly, the best path forward is to keep policies fueling the growth while enacting measures to address regional problems with far greater urgency and collaboration. This book was written in part as a call to action to federal, state, and local leaders to accelerate efforts to address the region's growing challenges before they lead to a true crisis. Can anyone manage life in Austin if a new drought of record reduces the Colorado River and Highland Lakes to a point where there is not enough water to meet people's basic needs? Major collisions already force law enforcement agencies to completely close the region's principal surface artery to treat victims and clear debris, turning a seventy-five-minute commute into an hours-long traffic jam on access roadways. Extreme weather events have repeatedly put the state's energy grid, which is not integrated with other states, at serious risk of failure. Will Texas suffer another Winter Storm Uri, as it did in 2021, when millions were left in frigid temperatures without power or water and more than 240 died from exposure, a number that public health officials consider a significant undercount?

For years now, the state's conservative elected leaders have waged war against big-city mayors and home rule authority. These continuing tensions, most visible in every biennial legislative session, stand in the way of the kind of state-local working groups that need to be formed and empowered to address the most pressing and urgent regional challenges.

Still, the attractive business climate and lifestyle of the emerging Austin–San Antonio megaregion isn't just a chamber of commerce pitch. Relative to the cost of living on the two coasts, Texas remains a bargain, and its economy is the envy of other states. The respected Milken Institute's annual survey of Best Performing Cities in 2024, which looks at a range of economic measures in the top two hundred cities by population in both the large and small categories, ranks the Austin–Round Rock metropolitan statistical area (MSA) as number one in the country, an improvement from its second-place finish in 2023. The San Antonio–New Braunfels MSA ranks number thirty-five, an impressive leap from number sixty-five only one year earlier.

Less visible, meanwhile, is the rapid growth of the corridor cities and those to the east and west of I-35 located along Interstate 10. Stop any American crossing a downtown street in a major East or West Coast city and ask them to name the fastest-growing cities in the United States. Few would correctly guess that seven of the fastest-growing fifteen US cities are in Texas, in numeric terms. Most non-Texans would struggle to find Georgetown, Kyle, Leander, and New Braunfels on a state map, all within a thirty-minute drive to either Austin or San Antonio. Georgetown, to Austin's northeast, was the fastest-growing city by percentage of population in 2021 and again in 2022, according to the US Census Bureau. Texas had three of the country's fastest-growing cities in terms of numeric population gain in 2022: Fort Worth was number one; San Antonio, third; and Austin, sixth. In 2023, Texas had seven of the fifteen fastest-growing US cities in numeric terms, according to the US Census Bureau, two in the Austin–San Antonio megaregion alone: San Antonio was number one; Fort Worth, number two; Houston, number seven; Georgetown, number eight; Celina, number nine; Fulshear, number eleven; and Denton, number thirteen.

The local economies of the corridor and adjacent cities are attracting new residents with affordability, good public schools, low crime rates, and new amenities. These cities have become home to more and more former big-city residents in search of more affordable housing and a slower-paced lifestyle while now commuting to jobs in the capital metro. In 2023, eight of the fifteen fastest-growing cities with more than twenty thousand residents, more than half of them, were in Texas, two in the Austin–San Antonio megaregion, Georgetown and Kyle (see table 1.1). Celina, Princeton, Anna, Prosper, and Forney are all in the DFW metro area. Fulshear is in the Houston metro, in Fort Bend County. The 2023 population numbers indicate much of the nation's and Texas' growth is in Texas suburbs.

Austin, often cited by graduating university students across the country as their number-one destination of choice for work and lifestyle, in 2022 surpassed San Jose, California, to take its place on the list of top ten US cities, according to 2023 Census Bureau data. In 2022, Texas became the first state in Census Bureau history to have four cities in the nation's top ten. Jacksonville, Florida, barely clipped Austin by fewer than six thousand residents, knocking Austin down to number eleven (see table 1.2). Still, Texas now has five cities among the top twelve: Houston (fourth), San

Table 1.1.
Top fifteen fastest-growing cities by percent among cities with
populations of more than twenty thousand, July 1, 2022–July 1, 2023

City	Percent increase	2022 population
1. Celina, Texas	26.6	43,317
2. Fulshear, Texas	25.6	42,616
3. Princeton, Texas	22.3	28,027
4. Anna, Texas	16.9	27,501
5. Lathrop, California	13.6	39,857
6. Centerton, Arkansas	11.2	23,953
7. Haines, Florida	10.8	37,272
8. Georgetown, Texas	**10.6**	**96,312**
9. Prosper, Texas	10.5	41,660
10. Forney, Texas	10.4	35,470
11. Kyle, Texas	**9.0**	**62,548**
12. Lebanon, Tennessee	8.9	48,112
13. Fort Mill, South Carolina	8.8	33,626
14. Leesburg, Florida	8.7	31,721
15. Athens, Ohio	8.6	24,673

Source: US Census Bureau.

Antonio (seventh), Dallas (ninth), Austin (eleventh), and Fort Worth (twelfth).

The Texas Triangle—formed by DFW to the north, Houston to the east, and Austin–San Antonio to the south—remains the number-one magnet nationally for the inflow of talented workers and their families. A remarkable number of people move for education or job opportunities within the Texas Triangle, according to the Texas Demographic Center (TDC) at the University of Texas at San Antonio. The center predicts such growth from out-of-state and in-state migration will continue apace for at least the next three decades.

Whereas the DFW and Houston metros each have populations of more than seven million people, the Austin and San Antonio

Table 1.2.

Top fifteen US cities by population, 2023

City	Population
1. New York City	8,258,035
2. Los Angeles	3,820,914
3. Chicago	2,664,452
4. Houston	2,314,157
5. Phoenix	1,650,070
6. Philadelphia	1,550,542
7. San Antonio	**1,495,295**
8. San Diego	1,388,320
9. Dallas	1,302,868
10. Jacksonville	985,843
11. Austin	**979,882**
12. Fort Worth	978,468
13. San Jose	969,655
14. Columbus	913,175
15. Charlotte	911,311

Source: US Census Bureau.

metros combined surpassed five million for the first time in 2022, according to the TDC. While the Houston and Dallas metro areas rank in the top five nationally, more people live in the Austin–San Antonio corridor than in any of the neighboring states of Oklahoma, Louisiana, and New Mexico. If Austin–San Antonio were a state, it would be the twenty-fifth largest.

For demographers tracking future political trends in what today is one of the most conservatively led states in the nation, the blue cities of Austin and San Antonio are now home to one million more people than in all of rural Texas, which remains the largest rural population in the nation. The Texas myth is a horseman driving cattle. The reality is a single-occupancy pickup truck or SUV, one of thousands crawling through traffic on I-35, bounded by office

A megaregion is an overlapping number of densely populated cities and counties that form a single identifiable region, such as New York–Philadelphia or DFW. Common characteristics include boundaries blurred by commerce, interurban population movements, and the growth of connecting and surrounding suburbs and so-called bedroom communities. A steady flow of residents, workers, and consumers all travel across these boundaries for employment, cultural engagement, access to educational institutions, and lifestyle attractions. Cities within a megaregion tend to maintain their own distinct identities while becoming integral communities within a single, very large metro area with a major population base. In this instance, Austin and San Antonio serve as anchor cities that are steadily growing into a single MSA.

towers, warehouses, strip centers, and fast-food outlets, sometimes no faster than a herd of cattle being moved to market. Texas is no longer the mythic state of the lone cowboy and the open prairie. It's the country's fastest-growing state, increasingly defined by its big cities, and the Austin–San Antonio region is the fastest growing of them all.

Switch from population totals within the city limits, which exclude each big city's surrounding suburbs and communities, to the Census Bureau list of MSAs, and the Texas rankings are reshuffled. DFW is fourth in the country; Houston is fifth. San Antonio–New Braunfels is twenty-fourth; Austin–Round Rock is twenty-sixth (see table 1.3).

In March 2024, the US Census Bureau released its national counties and metropolitan areas population growth rankings for the period between July 1, 2022, and July 1, 2023. The Austin metro grew by 50,105 people in the twelve-month period to an estimate of 2.47 million. The San Antonio metro population increased by 48,071 to 2.7 million. In all, the Austin–San Antonio megaregion grew by 98,176 people in the one-year period. That is equal to the addition of 269 people daily.

Table 1.3.

Top thirty US metropolitan statistical areas by population, ranked, 2022

Metroplex	Population
1. New York City, New York	19,498,249
2. Los Angeles, California	12,799,100
3. Chicago, Illinois	9,262,825
4. Dallas–Fort Worth, Texas	8,100,037
5. Houston, Texas	7,510,253
6. Atlanta, Georgia	6,307,261
7. Washington, DC	6,304,975
8. Philadelphia, Pennsylvania	6,246,160
9. Miami, Florida	6,183,199
10. Phoenix, Arizona	5,070,110
11. Boston, Massachusetts	4,919,179
12. Riverside, California	4,688,053
13. San Francisco, California	4,566,961
14. Detroit, Michigan	4,342,304
15. Seattle, Washington	4,044,304
16. Minneapolis–St. Paul, Minnesota	3,712,020
17. Tampa–St. Petersburg, Florida	3,342,963
18. San Diego, California	3,269,973
19. Denver, Colorado	3,005,131
20. Baltimore, Maryland	2,834,316
21. Orlando, Florida	2,817,933
22. Charlotte, North Carolina	2,805,115
23. St. Louis, Missouri	2,796,999
24. San Antonio–New Braunfels, Texas	**2,703,999**
25. Portland, Oregon	2,508,050
26. Austin–Round Rock, Texas	**2,473,275**
27. Pittsburgh, Pennsylvania	2,422,725
28. Sacramento, California	2,420,608
29. Las Vegas, Nevada	2,336,573
30. Cincinnati, Ohio	2,271,479

Source: US Census Bureau.

If we measure the dramatic growth of the Austin–Round Rock and the San Antonio–New Braunfels corridors, as the Census Bureau now defines the two markets, and envision them growing together as a single megaregion, the combined population of 5.18 million would place it slightly ahead of Phoenix–Mesa–Chandler, Arizona, currently the country's tenth-largest MSA. And, for reference, 5.18 million in the Austin–San Antonio megaregion is more people than the entire state of Louisiana at 4.57 million. If a state, the Austin–San Antonio megaregion would be the nation's twenty-fifth-largest state, just ahead of Alabama.

While San Antonio has 30 percent more people than Austin, the reverse is true for the size of the two economies. Austin years ago surpassed San Antonio in economic size. The Austin metro's gross domestic product (GDP) in 2022 was $193.63 billion, while the San Antonio metro's GDP was $163.06 billion. That adds up to a combined $356.69 billion. Put another way, the Austin–San Antonio regional economy is larger than the GDP of all but 42 of the 195 countries tracked by the World Bank.

As the two cities continue to grow closer, someone undoubtedly will come up with a name for the new region. DFW was made recognizable globally by the ascent of DFW International Airport, which served more than seventy-three million passengers in 2022. Yet no one mistakes Dallas for Fort Worth or Fort Worth for Dallas, two distinctly different cities. Both cities, along with more than two hundred other municipalities in the thirteen-county MSA, are joined together in a metro area of 7.6 million people and counting. The growth of DFW's largest satellite cities, notably Arlington and Irving, Richardson and Plano, Garland and Carrollton, Lewisville and McKinney, and Denton—all small cities in 1980—now account for more than 2 million of those residents.

Texas, with more than 31.95 million people, remains the fastest-growing state in the nation, second only in absolute size to California, with 38.94 million, which represents a drop of 138,400 people from 2021, a decline that began in 2020, driven by COVID-19 deaths, rising street crime, homelessness, and falling immigration and birth rates. California's population loss might strike some as minuscule, percentage-wise, yet the change is significant. For the first time in its history as a state, California is no longer growing. That cost it a congressional seat in the last census, while Texas gained a new seat. Florida, with 22 million people, and New York, with 20 million, are the next two most populated states. Given the singular rate of growth in Texas, it should come as no surprise that Austin and San Antonio and all the corridor cities and several in the surrounding area are on track to become the nation's next megaregion.

Austin and San Antonio and the many municipalities connecting and flanking them are increasingly joined as one great continuum along the hypertrafficked I-35 corridor from Pflugerville to Floresville. Where farm pastures with grazing cattle and shrinking ranchlands with barbed wire fences once divided the various towns and communities of Central Texas, today the commuter looks out at a seemingly endless vista of commercial development and suburban sprawl. Landscape has become cityscape.

Anyone with a Texas driver's license who regularly uses I-35 in the region knows it isn't just Austin and San Antonio driving the gridlock. All the region's communities contribute to the growing congestion, including Round Rock and Georgetown, north of Austin; San Marcos, New Braunfels, Buda, and Kyle between the two big metros; and Seguin to the east and Boerne to the west along I-10.

The San Antonio–New Braunfels MSA grew to 2.5 million, a 19.5 percent rate of growth, from 2010 to 2020, while the Austin–Round Rock MSA grew to nearly 2.4 million, an astonishing 33 percent growth rate, during the same decade. Population numbers, once commonly updated every decade, are now restated annually. TDC demographers predict Austin will surpass San Antonio in population sometime after 2040.

The two big-city mayors, Kirk Watson in Austin and recently departed Ron Nirenberg in San Antonio, recognize this tsunami of regional growth. Both have a clear-eyed view of the attendant opportunities and challenges. The question for these officeholders, urban planners, regional governmental organizations, and certainly state leaders, as well as the business community and everyone with a stake in the delivery of social services and community building, is this: Will the region's leaders come together to ensure that such growth generates greater prosperity and creates a higher quality of life for all?

As many note, the growth is unstoppable. If the two MSAs now count more than 5 million people, demographers expect that number to almost double by 2060. Reaching 2060 might seem like a lifetime away for some, including the authors, but in the grand scheme of the life of cities, it is not. 2050 is less than twenty-five years from the time this book was written, the same passage of time Austin and San Antonio have experienced since 1998.

This book about the coming Central Texas megaregion began as an examination of the astonishing growth numbers of all cities in the subject area. It soon evolved into a more in-depth look at the many opportunities and challenges that accompany such growth. While the region is one of the country's leading tech and employment hubs, it also has serious vulnerabilities noted here in this chapter and explored in greater detail in the chapters ahead. Texas ranks among the worst states for public school funding and public health funding and suffers the highest number of uninsured adults and children in the nation.

We authors and many of the people we interviewed are sounding the bell for leaders at the local, regional, state, and federal levels to come together to address the challenges and make the most of the economic and social opportunities. Committing new resources will be essential, and organizing new collaborative public-private entities seems to be the most effective way to make sure every city has a seat at the table and that state and regional leaders stay fully engaged. With a shared mission, the leadership of the Austin–San Antonio megaregion can generate tens of thousands of new jobs for a fast-growing workforce of skilled workers and create new levels of prosperity and equity spread fairly across the region and throughout its increasingly diverse and minority-majority population.

This book is not just for current and future policymakers. It's for everyone who calls home the region where Central Texas meets South Texas. Everyone with generational roots in the region and everyone making a new home here has a stake in the future. Change is going to happen, even if all we do is stand back and watch it. Or we can manage smart change, driven by visionary leaders setting aside geographic rivalries, political partisanship, and a growing state–big city divide. The time to roll up our sleeves and get to work is now.

Regional planning is complicated by the lack of a single entity that encompasses and embraces the entire region. Management of this growth is further complicated by political tensions between conservative Republicans, who control all statewide offices, and city leaders who are Democratic or run in nonpartisan elections in cities that vote blue. State leaders have consistently enacted laws diminishing home rule powers over annexation, setting tax rates, and exercising the authority to pass and enforce a broad range of local ordinances. The state and large cities have taken to civil courts of law to litigate such disputes. No one can pretend this standoff will not affect regional options to manage growth and finance critical infrastructure projects.

"The state of Texas will succeed as a powerhouse economically and quality of life–wise if it recognizes that the Texas economy is the sum of its regional parts," Mayor Watson said. "The state needs to provide the tools to those regional component parts to do what they do or at least get out of the way because those cities and regions are going to do what they need to do to be successful. One of the key factors [is that] each of those regions have their distinct personalities, distinct ways of being successful, and that's good. It offers people a choice of where they want to live and work."

Flash back to 1980 when San Antonio had a population of 949,000 and a small airport where most flights went through Dallas or Houston, while Austin was a laid-back capital city of 383,000—almost one in five residents were students, faculty, or employees of UT. Some long for those simpler days, particularly longtime residents in Austin, many of whom came for college and never left. Gleaming office and residential towers now stand shoulder to shoulder downtown and are home at the street level to upscale boutiques and expensive hotels and restaurants busy seven days a week. Even the food trucks in Austin have lines of customers waiting patiently for service. It's all happening so fast, the pink granite-domed capitol is barely visible now from most points downtown. Yet to the visitor, the "Keep Austin Weird" counterculture is still evident in smaller, older music clubs, landmark restaurants, and

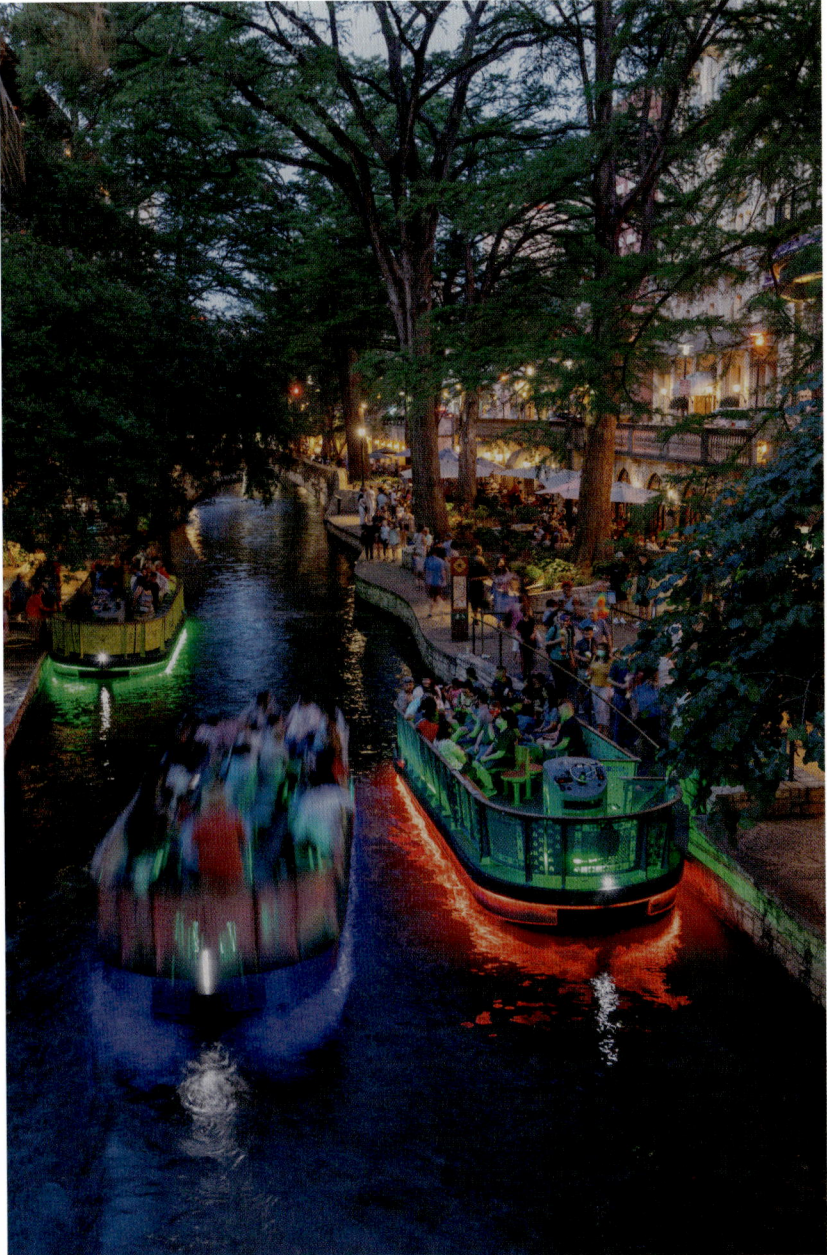

The San Antonio Paseo del Rio, or River Walk, glows at nighttime in the heart of downtown. Photo by Al Rendon.

The Texas State Capitol looms over Congress Avenue in downtown Austin.
Photo by Al Rendon.

locally owned shops tucked away inconspicuously in the shadow of the new high-tech, pricier Austin. The city wears its new wealth quite openly, but there is enough of old Austin still in the air to make it the coolest big town in Texas.

San Antonio has picked up momentum too. Many of its historic neighborhoods on the East and South Sides have gentrified as more young professionals flock to the urban core. San Antonio, once dubbed a brain drain city by demographers, gained attention as a very livable brain gain city by the time former Mayor Julián Castro declared the "Decade of Downtown" in 2010. Yet the essence of the state's major city that dates to the seventeenth century is found in its Spanish roots, Latino-majority population, and nineteenth-century German influences.

Each city can and should retain its unique culture and identity. San Antonio is older and more deliberate in its growth, while Austin is younger and moving faster. Sibling rivals, perhaps, but family nonetheless.

DFW and Houston will always be more populated than Austin–San Antonio and more global in their reach and will always boast larger-scale economies. But Austin–San Antonio is the heart of Texas. The Alamo, the Shrine to Texas Independence, is in San Antonio. The city celebrated its three hundredth anniversary in 2018, three years after its Spanish colonial missions and the Alamo were designated a UNESCO World Heritage Site. Austin has been the state capital since its founding in 1839. Together, the two cities form the cultural, historical, and governing center of the state.

Austin's skyline, many construction cranes, and high-velocity tech sector can overpower the sensibilities of longtime residents, yet the city remains defined in no small part by the University of Texas at Austin, state government, and the city's music and festival scene. Latino-dominant San Antonio—a city that has flown the flags of Spain, Mexico, the Republic, the Confederacy, and the Stars and Stripes—proudly guards its history, architecture, and bilingualism. Even today, highway signs mark the road mileage to San Antonio by noting the distance to the historic San Fernando Cathedral on Main Plaza, the oldest continuing functioning religious community in Texas.

"I think when you look at what is going on in the country and in the state of Texas, there's not a better area than what we have in San Antonio and Austin and in between. I really think it's a natural," said retired Major League Baseball pitcher Nolan Ryan, a Baseball Hall of Fame member who lives in Georgetown and works in offices next door to Round Rock's Dell Diamond stadium. Ryan holds ownership stakes in two minor-league baseball teams, the Round Rock Express and the San Antonio Missions. The Austin–San Antonio corridor has "the ability to expand with the amount of property around here. There's so many major corporations that have moved in here and want to headquarter here. I expect that to continue," Ryan added.

The region's growth rate will continue unchecked, sending the population total for the Austin–San Antonio region to 8.3 million people by 2050 and 9.6 million by 2060, according to TDC projections. What will it take for the federal government to redesignate the separate-but-adjoining Austin and San Antonio metro areas as a single MSA, as happened with Dallas and Fort Worth in 1973? The current answer is that a lot more people must live in one metro area and work in the other. Austin is the core city of a five-county metro, while San Antonio anchors an eight-county metro. The main dividing line is the border between Comal (San Antonio metro) and Hays (Austin metro) Counties. The federal rule observed and overseen by the US Office of Management and Budget, in cooperation with the US Bureau of Labor Statistics, is that 25 percent of the workforce must live in one adjoining metro and work in the other.

For example, someone who lives in New Braunfels in Comal County might be employed not far away in the collection of discount retail centers south of San Marcos in Hays County. Or a student at Texas State University in Hays County might be employed at the gigantic Buc-ee's gasoline station / retail complex in Comal County.

The current "employment interchange" between Austin and San Antonio, separated by seventy-five miles, isn't close to meeting the threshold for merging into one MSA. In 2016, a San Antonio Report analysis placed the ratio at 2.5 percent and concluded that an increase in the ratio is unlikely for two reasons. One impediment is I-35 congestion, making it increasingly difficult to travel between the region's cities in a predictable time frame.

A second reason is the almost zero interaction between fast-growing Williamson County, north of Austin, and the San Antonio metro cities. People living in Georgetown would find employment south of San Marcos to be a daunting commute, just as people living in Floresville, south of San Antonio, would find it unrealistic to commute to points north of New Braunfels.

That federal formula, however, might be rendered obsolete by enduring changes in employment and the workplace that grew out of the pandemic when remote work became a necessity. Since then, more workers have adopted hybrid work schedules. US cities have seen downtown office towers hollowed out as empowered workers have resisted returning to five-day office schedules. This dynamic remains in flux. Many employers are now pushing for employees to return to the office, while employees push back just as vigorously, unwilling to surrender newly won flexibility. The federal government could take note and modify the definition of a megaregion to reflect the existing reality on the ground.

Improved transportation is the key to facilitating worker mobility. Establishing reliable modern mass transit serving the corridor cities would make that possible. As the San Antonio Report analysis

I think the development of infrastructure is critically important, and that includes transportation infrastructure, utility infrastructure. This is a region that is growing because of quality of life. The vibrancy of the region is heavily dependent on how we manage our natural resources, most specifically water, because that is the vitality of this particular region. We obviously see the importance of the University of Texas at Austin to the growth of opportunity in Austin, Texas, and we now are starting to realize the importance of investing in our universities and our [community] college district in San Antonio. That needs to be part of our plan. That's important in how we develop skills training for our workforce and as we position ourselves for economic development as we move forward.

—Former San Antonio Mayor Ron Nirenberg

noted, the solutions could take decades. In the first decade of the 2000s, a regional planning group spent years attempting to establish a passenger rail service called the Lone Star Rail District using the same or parallel right-of-way owned by Union Pacific Railroad, a freight company. Both the rail district board and Union Pacific understood that freight traffic and passenger trains represented a dangerous mix. Union Pacific had too many industrial customers along its rail line parallel to I-35 to abandon it for a new, more circuitous line some miles to the east, perhaps tracking the State Highway 130 toll road. Having reached an impasse, the rail district's hopes died. The cost of building new tracks somewhere else was deemed prohibitive at the time. In retrospect, the $2 billion estimate seems small in the grand scheme of things. As *The New York Times* noted in an August 2023 article, the bipartisan Infrastructure Investment and Jobs Act passed by Congress and signed into law by President Biden in 2021 is serving to reignite stalled high-speed rail projects on both coasts and in Texas between Houston and Dallas.

Something large and sweeping must happen in the Austin–San Antonio region in terms of transportation to accommodate the growth that will arrive in the next three decades. It is hard to imagine a megaregion of eight million people functioning efficiently with only one central surface artery and no effective mass transit. People clamor for an alternative, but state leaders seem disconnected from the problem, and local leaders lack the resources to do much about it.

"I think [the growing consensus on collaboration] is really strong," added Ryan. "People realize that to accomplish some of these things, it would have to have the mindset to be willing to work outside their area for the betterment of the whole area. I would expect that."

In the chapters ahead, we take a much closer look at what makes Austin and San Antonio unique and distinct and at the commonalities we share that can ease the transition to growing together.

2

The Continuing Reinvention of Austin

We are the focal point of the worldwide knowledge economy. We have those great universities. It's no coincidence we are on the forefront of the creative economy.

—Austin Mayor Kirk Watson

My town, once celebrated for its laid-back weirdness, is now a turbocharged tech megalopolis being shaped by exiles from places like Silicon Valley.

—Texas journalist and longtime Austin resident Lawrence Wright, author of "The Astonishing Transformation of Austin" in the February 6, 2023, issue of *The New Yorker*

No US city has redefined itself more visibly and changed or grown faster than Austin while still clinging to its singular culture and identity. The ever-expanding Third Coast tech hub, with its rising downtown skyline of skyscrapers, still retains much of the counterculture charm that has attracted generations of young people to live, work, and play there. Even as Cybertrucks start to roll off the assembly line at Tesla's Giga-Texas factory, the company's 2,500-acre production site on the Colorado River east of the city, a recent *New York Times* article celebrated the thousands of locals who flock to Barton Springs in the city's center, what the *Times* called "an oasis in the middle of a scorching Texas summer." While much of the country sheltered in air-conditioned spaces through a sweltering summer of record heat in 2023, the *Times* pictured a communal gathering of Austinites sunning themselves after a bracing plunge into the

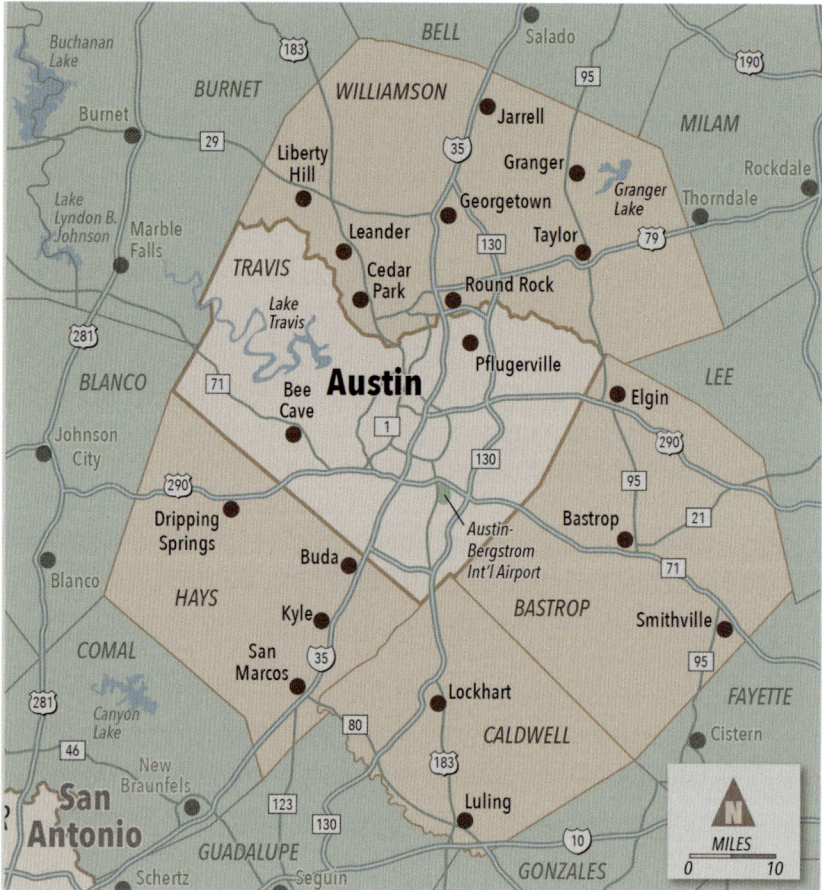

The five counties of the Austin metropolitan statistical area: Bastrop, Caldwell, Hays, Travis, and Williamson. Map by Mike Fisher.

three-acre pool's spring-fed waters. Protected by successive generations, Barton Springs remains the crown jewel of 358-acre Zilker Park and a symbol of all that longtime residents hope never to lose to development. A panorama of gleaming towers and building cranes serves as a backdrop in social media images, a reminder that Austin's oasis lies in the heart of its booming economy.

Longtime Austinites who experienced the city in the 1960s and '70s lament its seemingly overnight evolution from a small, less ambitious city with a laid-back counterculture to one of the fastest-growing urban destinations in the country. It's true that the "Keep Austin Weird" bumper stickers are now faded, and the stately, pink-domed Texas Capitol is no longer visible from all four points of the compass. Yet Austin retains its charm. The city that is home to state government and the globally recognized University of Texas (UT) continues to be a magnet for new generations of youth and talent drawn to good jobs and a great lifestyle.

As more and more people compete for jobs and housing in Austin, with home prices rising significantly each year, the outflow and overflow of people are adding to the growth in the suburban cities and small towns surrounding the state capital. What might be unwanted growth to longtime Austinites—who lament the loss of landmark music venues, bars, and restaurants—serves as a catalyst for attracting even more newcomers drawn by all the buzz.

As city boosters boast, Austin surpassed San Jose, the capital of Silicon Valley, to become the tenth-largest US city in 2022. Austin fell back to number eleven in 2023, surpassed by Jacksonville by fewer than 6,000 residents. But for twelve consecutive years from 2010 to 2022, the Austin–Round Rock–Georgetown metro area was the fastest-growing region in the country among large metros, according to US Census data. The Austin metro area added almost 63,000 residents between 2021 and 2022, growing at a rate of 2.7 percent. Put another way, Austin welcomed 173 newcomers to the area each and every day that year. Between 2022 and 2023, the Austin metro added 50,105 people, or 137 people daily, reaching a five-county total of 2.47 million people.

More than 383,000 people resided in Austin in 1980 when the legendary Armadillo Music Headquarters staged its last concert before an audience of 1,500 in the former National Guard armory where an office tower now stands. Today, with just less than 1 million people living in Austin proper and 2.35 million living in the Austin–Round Rock metro area, the annual Austin City Limits Music Festival attracts 450,000 concertgoers over two weekends in October. Another 300,000 attend the South by Southwest (SXSW) music festival and conferences that overtake the city for ten days every March, as musicians from around the world look to break through and tech leaders, film industry executives, and Hollywood stars convene. Austin is a profoundly changed city, yet the music hasn't died.

Austin's transformation did not happen overnight, even if it feels that way to lifers yearning for times gone by. The truth is, Austin's evolution from a quiet, easygoing capital city with a mellow, small-town feel really began in the 1980s when the first wave of tech companies arrived, even as the city's culture continued to flourish alongside the emergence of a tech sector. The formation of the private equity firm Austin Ventures, for example, gained national attention as it raised nearly $4 billion and established ten venture capital funds. At the same time, Whole Foods supermarkets were born out of the natural-food movement in the city. Austin remains a place that retains its unique place in the state, where the politics are progressive and the beckoning shade and jogging paths encircling Lady Bird Lake offer an urban nature experience few cities can match. The scenic Texas Hill Country, with its quaint German towns and sparkling rivers, is easily reached west of Austin. For those thriving in contemporary Austin, the city's ambiance remains a major calling card.

Today, Austin is two cities: first, an ever-diminishing population of people who lived there in the 1970s and '80s and lament the city's unchecked growth and newfound wealth, and second, the seemingly incessant in-migration of young professionals filling thousands of new tech jobs at companies like International Business Machines (IBM), Dell, Freescale, Advanced Micro Devices (AMD), Samsung, Solectron Texas, Applied Materials, and Oracle, not to mention Facebook, Google, Apple, and Tesla. Billionaire tech moguls by the dozen now call Austin home, their private jets hangared at Austin-Bergstrom International Airport (ABIA), where commercial travelers can catch nonstop flights to multiple European cities and other international destinations.

People fleeing cities like New York and San Francisco consider Austin a bargain, but they don't tell that to the locals. The steep rise in housing costs is causing others to depart the city. Austin's neighborhoods east of I-35, along the segregated side of town that has long been home to marginalized communities of color, have experienced significant gentrification in the last two decades. Every week now, as hundreds of new residents arrive in Austin, a smaller wave of residents pack up and leave for more affordable cities and towns in the region, places like Lockhart, Leander, Buda, and Kyle, all growing fast in their own right. Meanwhile, new office and residential towers, one outdoing the other in design and height, keep going up as construction cranes stand sentinel all along the downtown horizon. Leave Austin for six months, and you'll see a different city on your next visit—after you fight your way in through the congested highway traffic on and around I-35.

"People may have their mortgage paid off. But they can't pay the property taxes because the appraisals are going up so high, because everything around them is going up," observed state Rep. Sheryl Cole of Austin on the negative effects of gentrification occurring in portions of the city.

If old-timers mark the beginning of the end of vintage Austin four decades or more ago, the architects of the new Austin will look back at the same years and see the birth of a new era of prosperity: Austin metro as a fast-growing tech hub.

Austin downtown construction in 2024, adding to an already dramatic skyline. Photo by Al Rendon.

Austin's tech scene can be traced to the arrival of retired US Navy Admiral Bob Inman, who earlier served as deputy director of the CIA under President Ronald Reagan. Inman was chosen to lead a consortium of major computer and semiconductor manufacturers in 1983 and establish what became known as the Microelectronics and Computer Consortium (MCC) to challenge Japanese market penetration in the semiconductor industry, just as the United States and the rest of the world were moving into the age of personal computers. Leading US advanced manufacturing and aeronautic companies agreed to join the consortium to counter the growing Japanese market share in the chip market. Inman presided over a multicity competition for MCC's headquarters.

He later told the *New Yorker* staff writer Lawrence Wright that San Antonio made the most impressive pitch, but the lack of a Tier One research university ruled out the city. At the time, the University of Texas at San Antonio was barely one decade old and still a relatively unknown commuter school. Austin surprisingly beat out its East Coast and West Coast rivals, thanks in no small part to a $2 billion package of state incentives. The nucleus of a tech sector was created. Austin also overcame considerable resistance from environmentalists who opposed the rapid growth and change. New commercial developments were approved, even those that obscured views of the venerable state capitol building. Former Texas Gov. John Connally and former Lt. Gov. Ben Barnes launched ambitious development plans there and elsewhere around the state, although the savings-and-loan crisis that landed hard in Texas in the late 1980s caused their overleveraged businesses to collapse from within and brought a hiatus to development in Austin and other Texas cities for some years.

Yet Austin's tech sector continued to grow with the arrival of AMD and the success of a UT student named Michael Dell, whose dorm room start-up would eventually turn into Dell Computers, which helped lead the PC revolution and would make the UT drop-out a billionaire many times over. Today, UT's Dell Medical School bears his name, and he has become a high-profile investor in the San Antonio Spurs, which now play multiple games each season in Austin.

Even before the arrival of MCC in 1983 and a microchip consortium called Sematech in 1988, IBM had operated a typewriter assembly plant in Austin since 1967. The company transformed itself first via mainframe computer systems, then PCs, IT services, and cloud computing, and now AI technologies. Texas Instruments, then a calculator company and now a major player in the semiconductor space, also opened in Austin in 1967. Motorola arrived a few years later. By the time Inman and MCC arrived, the seeds of a thriving tech sector had been planted and were flourishing.

Austin Ventures quickly became the state's leading venture capital firm, seeding the growth of hundreds of tech ventures large and small. In short, Austin became Silicon Hills, the Texas version of California's Silicon Valley. The dot-com bust rattled Austin's economic development leaders, who organized Opportunity Austin in 2003 to accelerate efforts to recruit tech companies in search of an attractive workforce in a business-friendly state. Austin also boasted enviable lifestyle credentials, marketing itself as the music capital of the country. The proactive strategy worked more than anyone could have imagined. In April 2024, for example, South Korea's Samsung Electronics Co. announced it would raise its total investment in the Austin area to a total of $44 billion for chip manufacturing and an advanced packaging hub, including an existing $17 billion chip plant announced in 2021 in Taylor, near Austin. The increased Samsung investment, according to *The Wall Street Journal* and Bloomberg News, would receive incentives, perhaps $6 billion, from the 2022 federal CHIPS and Science Act.

Today, more than 1,500 tech companies operate in the city. The companies feed off the steady supply of skilled graduates from the University of Texas at Austin (UT-Austin), the flagship campus of the UT System statewide. It had a record enrollment of 53,082 students in 2023 and consistently ranks among the top ten public universities in the country.

Austin higher education extends beyond UT. Austin Community College's enrollment is more than 70,000 students. The city has three private universities: St. Edward's University (2,760 students), Concordia University Texas (1,707 students), and the city's historically Black college, Huston-Tillotson University (990 students).

Students and young professionals have come to the city for more than good jobs. The weekly alternative newspaper, *The Austin Chronicle*, dreamed up the idea of showcasing the city's vibrant music scene by launching an annual festival they called South by Southwest, first staged in 1987. To say the festival grew quickly would be an understatement. The creatives who formed SXSW believed Austin could match Nashville or Los Angeles for music and creativity but needed to have its story shared more widely. Within a decade, it had become the premier gathering of creatives in the country, spreading from music to film and all things tech. SXSW put Austin on the global map. All that growth is visible from the heavily trafficked highways leading into Austin, which now features a downtown skyline surpassed only by Houston and Dallas.

"A big part of what I was saying in my first time as mayor, which was 1997 to 2001, was that Austin's downtown wasn't much of a downtown. We didn't have a convention center hotel, for example," Austin Mayor Kirk Watson recalled. "We needed to build one, and we did. We doubled the size of our convention center. What I was saying is we couldn't have a downtown based on the older economy, lawyers, real estate, and bankers. We needed the new economy that was growing up in Austin."

Watson's dream of a revitalized downtown was realized even bigger and faster than he imagined. Not everyone is happy about that. The longtime Austin resident, book author, and *New Yorker* staff writer Lawrence Wright recalled an experience from 2022 when he was invited to induct Texas music legend Joe Ely into the Austin City Limits Music Hall of Fame. Wright and his wife, Roberta, left their home in the historic Tarrytown neighborhood for a night in the swanky W Hotel tower next to the Moody Theatre after the gala induction ceremony. Gazing out from their high-rise room, Wright wrote, "When Roberta opened the blinds, we had a sensation known to every longtime resident: we had no idea where we were. It was difficult even to discern what direction we were facing, because skyscrapers blocked the horizon. Ten building cranes were visible from that one window."

Given how few of the city's one million people were born and raised in Austin, many might not know its origin story. It's always been a special place with ample water and green spaces—"the beautiful canvas God gave us to paint," in the words of Opportunity Austin founder Gary Farmer. Austin will turn two hundred years old in 2039. Maribeau B. Lamar, the incoming president of the fledgling Republic of Texas, founded a speck of a hamlet called Waterloo along the Colorado River in 1837. Lamar liked the site's natural beauty so much that he made it the capital of the new Republic of Texas. In 1839, the name was changed to Austin, honoring the colonialist leader Stephen F. Austin.

An initial street grid was designed for the site by Lamar's friend Edwin Waller, who later became Austin's first mayor and namesake for Waller Creek, which feeds into the Colorado River. Like the river, the decades flowed by. State government offices expanded, including the capitol building constructed between 1875 and 1888, which is taller than the US Capitol building by 14.64 feet. That and the establishment of the UT in 1883 cemented Austin's future, though no one could have predicted it would grow to become the tenth-largest US city.

For newcomers, Austin's early history isn't central to their arrival. It's a city of opportunity, perhaps the leading destination in the country for coastal exiles fleeing high living costs as well as young graduates drawn to high-paying tech jobs. Austin is still a city where it's fun to be young as long as your paycheck is sufficient to handle the fast-rising costs of housing and the city's upscale culinary and entertainment scene.

For those who can't afford to keep pace with residential prices, the answer probably lies somewhere south along I-35 in fast-growing bedroom communities like Kyle or farther east to Lockhart. Some of those priced out of Austin have found work and new homes in San Antonio. One truth about the Austin–San Antonio megaregion is this: One way or another, there is room for everybody, and that's why it seems everyone is coming.

"There is no way you can talk about Austin over the past twenty-five years and not immediately think of the words *growth* and *rapid growth*. Austin has always been growing, always learning and knowing success," Watson said. "The past twenty-five years, the rapid growth on top of the growth that already was occurring has made significant changes. It shifted the imagination and the minds of people.

"Austin was well situated to be that place, especially as people, because of technology, could live anywhere they wanted to live and access labor, capital, and markets any day with the push of a button," Watson continued.

According to US Census Bureau data, the Austin metro ranked as follows for numeric and percentage population growth, respectively, from 2010 to 2019:

- Number eight in the nation, with a 510,760 gain.

- Number three in the nation, with a 29.8 percent gain.

Austin's metro area continues to accelerate and reached 2.47 million people in 2023. The Austin metro surpassed the San Antonio metro in payrolls in January 2018, despite San Antonio having 250,000 more people (see table 2.1).

Austin has a larger share of its workforce in the sixteen-to-sixty-four age range than San Antonio, where more people are younger or older.

Table 2.1.

Payroll employment by metro, September 2024

Metroplex	Payroll employment
Austin	1,354,500
San Antonio	1,180,500

Source: Federal Reserve Bank of Dallas.

Table 2.2.

Per capita personal income by metro, 2022

Metroplex	Per capita personal income
Austin	$75,119
San Antonio	$55,180

Source: US Bureau of Economic Analysis.

"It is the focus on talent," Watson said. "It is how you attract and retain the talent of people you want for all these different industries—Facebook, Google, and others."

Austin's per capita income is significantly higher than San Antonio's (see table 2.2). This stems from the capital city's higher educational attainment. While 55.1 percent of adults over age twenty-five have four-year degrees in Austin, only 27.2 percent of adults have four-year degrees in San Antonio. Actually, much of Austin's population consists of people from elsewhere who attended UT, fell in love with Austin, and never left. Austin's higher incomes partially explain why ABIA has more international and domestic nonstop routes than San Antonio International Airport.

With growth, traffic congestion has become an acute problem, partly because local voters in the 1990s and early 2000s turned down transportation bond proposals. Public opinion has since changed. In 2022, Austin voters approved packages of transportation projects totaling more than $20 billion. The projects, if completed, will add a new, lower level to I-35 downtown and add managed lanes aimed at improving vehicular flow. Light-rail and bus options will be expanded too. In 2023, the Austin City Council approved initial funding for the design of lower, wider lanes of I-35 in the city, along with decks and wider bridges in a program called Cap and Stitch. A light-rail is planned between the Austin airport and the downtown convention center, which will be expanded and heightened at a projected cost of $1.6 billion.

The higher cost of housing in Austin has led to affordability and homelessness problems that city leaders are struggling to address. By 2023, housing had grown so expensive that newly hired UT-Austin professors said they could only afford to live in distant neighborhoods, requiring long commutes. For students, housing issues are even more acute.

"Our emergency service workers can't afford to live in the city," Cole said. "We need them to live inside the city."

"You don't want your police, fire, and EMS personnel living fifty miles from where they work," added Farmer. "You don't want your teachers having to commute an hour to get to an elementary school to teach your kids."

I-35, running north and south through the city, has long served as a geographic and racial and ethnic dividing line defining, in effect, two Austins. A person driving north through Austin from, say, San Antonio toward Dallas would see the two Austins easily. To the left, the west side, is the prosperous Austin consisting of the state capitol and numerous state government buildings, along with downtown Austin's high-rise offices, hotels, and condominium towers. Adjacent to downtown dwells UT-Austin, with its historic Main Building tower, the looming football stadium, and a developing medical school complex. Just beyond the campus, to the west, sits a new generation of student housing. The city's most expensive neighborhoods lie farther west and northwest of downtown.

To the right of I-35, east of the highway and just north of Lady Bird Lake, the landscape is noticeably flatter, and not just because some of the land plots are cemeteries. The eastern neighborhoods

The Texas Longhorns face off with the Alabama Crimson Tide at Darrell K Royal–Texas Memorial Stadium in September 2022. With an official seating capacity of 100,119, the stadium is the seventh largest in the United States. Photo by David Hendricks.

there historically were for the working class, especially for Hispanics and Blacks. Significant gentrification has occurred in recent decades, with wealthier residents moving across the highway to the east, modifying and updating housing, and adding mixed-use developments, all of which raised property values and taxes, pricing out older residents. It's easy to see the difference from the I-35 geographic divide—wealth creation to the west and a vintage, lower-income Austin to the east that is steadily losing ground to the expansion of corporate Austin. The divide cuts deeper in another way. While longtime residents might acknowledge the corporate newcomers and the high-paying jobs they bring, they are not happy to see residents driven out of East Austin's Latino enclave. They also are unhappy to see Austin's traditionally liberal politics challenged by the arrival of libertarian tech billionaires and the influence on politics they might have on the city and their workforces. Many longtime residents appreciate the continuing waves of new jobs but lament how the city they know and love is changing.

Mexican American working-class families and others long rooted east of I-35 are seeking more affordable housing in places like Kyle and Buda. Austin's newest residents seem oblivious to the two changing narratives, one of vintage Austin, the other of Austin's barrio. The waves of young tech workers who migrated to Austin to be part of "Silicon Hills" have little interest in those claiming Austin's gains also are responsible for what Austin is losing. The migrants might not even live in Austin proper, preferring the rapidly growing northern suburbs of Cedar Creek and Pflugerville, but their presence is felt all across the city.

This partial merging underway between the two sides of I-35 causes tension. Resistance has risen with the goal of preserving the cultural and ethnic character of the East Side neighborhoods with their bilingual gathering places. But the gentrification trend continues, creating housing and equity issues local leaders are hard-pressed to address.

Housing "is a multiple-faceted issue. A whole lot of money, in terms of bonds, has been passed [to] build more housing in a place that is growing and has an impact on supply and demand," Watson said. "Second, we passed an ordinance to start the process of building more transit-oriented development along the new rail system, making it denser and more successful. The voters decided to build the new light-rail system and set aside more than $300 million to avoid displacement [of residents] along that."

It wasn't just traffic and housing where population growth created urban challenges. About a decade ago, Austin found it had outgrown its health-care capabilities. An effort was mounted to create a medical school at UT-Austin as a catalyst for greater access to health care.

"It never made sense to me . . . why Austin, Texas, with a world-renowned, Tier One research university that has made such a difference, didn't have its own medical school," Watson said. "There are historical reasons why the medical school was in Galveston. To solve the funding puzzle, we brought in the local health-care district, one of the major private providers, and worked with the regents of the UT System and the university itself, and we were able to get a medical school, a new twenty-first-century teaching hospital and safety net hospital. We were able to offer clinical care. It puts us into a different industry."

The new UT-Austin medical school also proved something else. "Our citizens have been very willing to invest in their futures," Watson explained. "Travis County voted to increase their property taxes to invest in the medical school. And when it comes to transportation, they [voters] haven't turned us down in quite a while."

Additional critical infrastructure for water and energy—to address expected population growth and to avert the massive interruptions in service experienced during Winter Storm Uri in 2021—are being explored but not yet implemented.

Austin's water dependence on the Colorado River and Highland Lakes puts it at risk if and when another record drought occurs.

Austin has a stable, thriving base of public and private employment (see table 2.3).

Technology companies abound in Austin. Those with more than six thousand employees each include Samsung, Austin Semiconductor, Apple, and IBM.

The annual growth of jobs in Austin has outpaced new housing starts, which has driven up house prices dramatically (see

Table 2.3.

Austin top employers, approximate levels, 2022

Employer	Approximate level
State government	60,000
University of Texas at Austin	24,000
City and county government	19,000
H-E-B grocery chain	13,500
Dell Inc.	13,000
Federal government	13,000
Austin Independent School District	12,200
St. David's HealthCare Partnership	10,300
Ascension Seton	10,000

Source: Austin Chamber of Commerce.

table 2.4). The cost of housing in Austin in 2022 was 22 percent higher than the national average, according to the US Bureau of Economic Analysis. Also in 2022, only 30 percent of houses for sale were affordable in the Austin area for people earning a median income. The trend appears to be a long-term phenomenon. No one expects a slowdown in housing price escalations.

The growth in population, jobs, and incomes has changed Austin's character over the years. In the eyes of many, Austin has become so technology- and corporate-driven that *Texas Monthly* magazine, based in Austin, stated in a 2022 cover story that Austin had become unrecognizable.

Newcomers, especially those from out of state, have not been held back by the state's conservative restrictions. It doesn't seem

Table 2.4.

Metro housing prices, May 2022

Metroplex	Average housing price	Median housing price
Austin	$680,386	$550,000
San Antonio	$388,294	$339,317

Source: Texas A&M University's Texas Real Estate Center.

to matter much to them. What matters is that Austin has become a city of opportunity in an innovative, sky-is-the-limit atmosphere.

"We have to start with equity, making sure Austin is a place everyone can enjoy," Watson stressed. "I want our economic development paradigm to be different," he added. "Instead of counting the number of jobs we've created—and I want to keep creating those jobs—I want to talk about how many Austinites we can get into those jobs and how we train them to get them into those jobs. Early childhood development and day care is often the second-biggest cost to households. It makes a difference on when and where people can work."

Austin and the Texas Longhorns football team seem to share the same motto: "All gas, no brakes."

The San Antonio Story

Even as San Antonio has become one of the country's fastest-growing cities, it has taken care to preserve its history and culture. From frontier days to the present, San Antonio has been a destination city for visitors who want to experience where history was made. It's a city whose early founding by Spanish colonialists, role in fighting for Texas independence, and importance as home to multiple military installations have given it a character unlike any other city in the Southwest. Millions of visitors come annually to enjoy the city's storied Paseo del Rio, the famous River Walk; the Alamo and the nineteenth-century Spanish missions; and the many other amenities and attractions. San Antonio is a big city with a small-town feel. Visitors say it's a place where they instantly feel welcome.

San Antonians savor how the past informs the present, most evident today in the ongoing redevelopment of the Alamo Plaza and the city's UNESCO World Heritage designation, accorded in 2015, which recognizes the "outstanding universal value" of the five eighteenth-century Spanish colonial missions, including the Alamo. San Antonio also has won recognition from UNESCO as a destination World Heritage City of Gastronomy for its diverse culinary culture.

The San Antonio Conservation Society and other organizations have worked to successfully protect and preserve historic buildings, and the city has come to recognize the importance of its

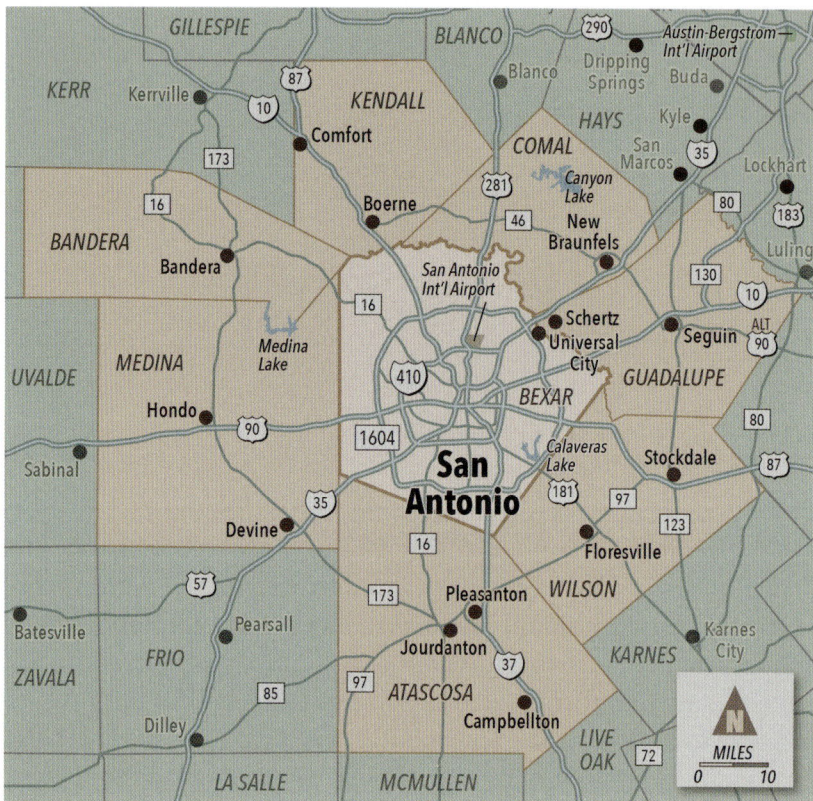

The eight counties of the San Antonio metropolitan statistical area: Atascosa, Bandera, Bexar, Comal, Guadalupe, Kendall, Medina, and Wilson. Map by Mike Fisher.

prehistory when Indigenous tribes and communities were drawn to its abundant natural springs, nut-bearing trees, and wild game. Archaeologists have found evidence of hunter-gatherer habitation dating back at least twelve thousand years. People have found home in Yanaguana, the Indigenous name meaning "place of eternal springs and waters," probably for as long as humans have dwelled on the continent.

Early explorers, followed by settlers from Europe, made their way here hundreds of years ago. San Antonio celebrated its three hundredth anniversary in 2018, founded in 1718 when the first mission and presidio were established at San Pedro Springs. The city's name is even older, dating to June 13, 1691, the feast day of St. Anthony of Padua, when a small Spanish expedition crossed what they named the Rio San Antonio. No other large Texas city can claim to have flown six flags: Spain, France, Mexico, the Republic, the Confederacy, and finally, the Stars and Stripes.

The Alamo started out as something else: Mission San Antonio de Valero, originally located on San Pedro Creek, its adobe walls soon washed away in floods. A sturdier limestone mission was then erected at the Alamo's current site, though never finished. It was the first of five Spanish Catholic missions built along the San Antonio River to house, convert, and educate the Indigenous population in Western ways after similar efforts by the Spanish to establish the missions in East Texas failed. In 1810, Mexico broke away from Spanish control. While a newly independent government slowly took shape in distant Mexico City, Anglo settlers from the United States were brought west into faraway Tejas by Stephen F. Austin and other colonizers. The settlers wanted to own slaves, but Mexico changed its constitution to forbid the practice, so the Tejanos rebelled.

The initial military resistance failed after the 1813 Battle of Medina. The battle took the lives of half the registered males in San Antonio and led the Spanish to exact revenge by herding hundreds of women and children into imprisonment, where soldiers engaged in mass violations. Mexico would gain its independence from Spain in 1821, but the spirit of rebellion and quest for independence in Texas persisted and eventually led to the 1836 Battle of the Alamo, converted into a defensive fort some decades after the mission was deconsecrated by Catholic authorities. The Alamo defenders—greatly outnumbered, armed with little gunpowder, and exhausted after the thirteen-day siege—were overrun. Gen. Antonio López de Santa Anna, Mexico's supreme leader, ordered the execution of any survivors. Meanwhile, in the forested northeast reaches of Texas, Houston trained another Texas militia. One month after the fall of the Alamo, Houston defeated Santa Anna's army at San Jacinto, near the present-day city of Houston. Texas became a republic, with San Antonio its largest city. San Antonio became known as the Alamo City. Today, the Alamo is the

The famed Alamo Church is the main attraction at San Antonio's downtown Alamo Plaza, which in 2024 was undergoing redevelopment aimed at adding historical context about the 1836 battle for plaza visitors. Photo by Al Rendon.

single most visited site in Texas, attracting more than 2.5 million visitors each year.

An appreciation of the military is embedded in San Antonio's DNA from its very founding through Texas independence and onward. In 1859, two years before the start of the American Civil War, the US Army established the San Antonio Arsenal along the banks of the San Antonio River. Scouting and expeditionary patrols that left San Antonio to replenish and strengthen isolated forts farther out West were outfitted at the Arsenal, which would be surrendered by its Union commander to Confederate forces without a shot being fired in 1861.

After the Confederates surrendered at Appomattox in 1865, the US Army returned to San Antonio and expanded the twenty-one-acre Arsenal as the United States pressed farther westward to secure the vast lands wrested from Mexico in the 1848 Treaty of Guadalupe. The agreement, which Mexico signed under duress, moved the Texas-Mexico border south to the Rio Grande and included its surrender of a vast swath of territory that today includes Texas, New Mexico, southwestern Colorado, Arizona, Utah, Nevada, and California.

San Antonio's central role in the eventual taming of the Comancheria, the vast southwestern reaches controlled by the Comanches through the 1880s, has always been an underappreciated chapter in the city's post–Civil War history. The army finally closed the Arsenal after World War II. In 1985, grocery store heir Charles Butt moved Corpus Christi–based H-E-B to San Antonio and installed its new headquarters at the Arsenal. Today, H-E-B is the largest privately held grocery company in the country, with more than 145,000 employees, and the state's largest private employer. The historic campus has been significantly expanded.

The military presence here grew with the late nineteenth-century establishment of Fort Sam Houston on the high ground northeast of the city. By World War I, it was the largest army post in the country. By the end of World War II, the army designated Fort Sam as its primary medical training facility. The construction of Brooke Army Medical Center (BAMC) included the world-renowned Burn Center.

San Antonio also played a key role in the establishment of military aviation in the early twentieth century with the 1916 founding of Kelly Field. The US Army Air Corp facilities eventually expanded into a major air force presence: Kelly Air Force Base (Kelly AFB), Lackland Air Force Base (Lackland AFB), Brooks Air Force Base (Brooks AFB), and Randolph Field. By the mid-twentieth century, the US military was a pillar of the San Antonio economy.

The Mexican Revolution sent waves of Spanish-speaking refugees to San Antonio in the second decade of the 1900s. Many settled west of downtown in unplatted neighborhoods, forced to live in squalor in *jacales*, small shanties constructed of scavenged construction materials: corrugated metal, wood, and even cardboard. Few households had running water or indoor plumbing. City fathers passed bonds to construct public sewer systems in the central city and surrounding neighborhoods to the north, but the *barrio* and citizens of Mexican descent were purposely neglected. Crowded, unhealthy collections of jacales were precariously perched along creek beds prone to destructive flooding. Many families shared a common outhouse and outdoor water spigot. Day laborers toiled for wages that kept them impoverished.

In 1921, the worst flood in city history left downtown buildings under twenty feet of water. City police and firefighters were ill-equipped to mount a strong rescue response, so army soldiers from Fort Sam Houston assumed control. The real suffering occurred on the West Side, where creek beds were deluged with floodwaters and countless victims were swept away, including many children and elderly unable to escape the unexpected inundation. The official death count was placed at eighty, but authorities declined to count the hundreds of missing whose bodies were carried far downriver and never recovered. To this day, no memorial exists remembering the lives of so many Mexican Americans swept to their deaths, in no small part because of the Anglo ruling class and its inhumane treatment of people living in the West Side barrio.

Such conditions of squalor and neglect persisted as city officials expanded construction of the Olmos Dam, visible today from Texas Hwy. 281, which runs north and south through San Antonio. The larger dam and other flood-control investments protected the near–North Side neighborhoods and downtown's central business district but did nothing to make the West Side any safer. A 1952 edition of *Look* magazine, which each week reached four million US households, devoted page after page of text and photos to the deep poverty and segregation that Mexican Americans in San Antonio and south to the border were forced to endure, the direct result of official local government policies of disinvestment, redlining, and segregation. It was as if the established civic and business interests that defined local government in the late nineteenth century and through the first seven decades of the twentieth century regarded San Antonians of Mexican descent as a lesser people, unworthy of equal access to public education, medical and health care, public infrastructure, and employment opportunities. Even today, the long-term impact of the second-class treatment of minority communities can be measured in a single statistic: San Antonio's inner-city neighborhoods include more than one hundred miles of streets without sidewalks, tree canopy, and good lighting, according to the city government. Life expectancy in some parts of the inner city, home to minority communities, is twenty years less than in more affluent North Side zip codes.

After the devastating flood of 1921 and others that followed, conservationists saved the downtown segment of the San Antonio River so that it later could be developed into a downtown park with a walkway. River Walk construction began in 1933 as part of President Franklin Roosevelt's Works Progress Administration. Tourism expanded the San Antonio economy, particularly as roadways improved and automobile travel became more affordable and popular among American families eager to explore all parts of Texas. Even today, 70 percent of the tens of millions of people who visit San Antonio each year arrive by automobile. A longtime promotional line is "Every Texas has two homes: where they live and San Antonio."

The civil rights movement, started by Mexican Americans in 1929 in Corpus Christi with the formation of the League of United Latin American Citizens (LULAC), scored early victories throughout South Texas, desegregating schools, hotels, barbershops, lunch counters, and other retail venues as well as public amenities such as community pools and water fountains. Americans are far more familiar with the sacrifices made by Blacks than the long struggle by people of Mexican descent to win equal rights and justice in Texas and the Southwest.

That movement was accelerated as World War II came to a close in 1945, bringing profound changes in San Antonio and South Texas as returning servicemen of Mexican descent asserted their rights under the GI Bill. LULAC supported the 1948 founding of the GI Forum, also in Corpus Christi, by Dr. Hector Garcia, a decorated army major. The organizations established chapters in San Antonio and the Rio Grande Valley. Mexican American GIs and a growing number of sympathetic Anglos called for equal treatment at the polls, lunch counters, hospital wards, public parks, and pools. Reformers campaigned for the right of people of color to own property in the many neighborhoods where deed restrictions and other covenants kept out Mexican Americans and Blacks. Even some of San Antonio's cemeteries were segregated.

The gains reformers made were dramatic for the times yet modest in retrospect. San Antonio would continue to grow as one of the most economically segregated cities in the country, where access to education and opportunity would largely be defined by where you lived and the color of your skin.

As the decades passed and Dallas and Houston surpassed San Antonio in size and ambition, it became clear that military installations and the city's modest tourism sector were not enough to sustain a major city. HemisFair '68, a world's fair focused on the Americas, was organized by civic and business leaders to attract newfound attention to the city and kick-start the economy with a message to nations south of the border that San Antonio was a multicultural city deserving of greater recognition throughout the hemisphere. The city went to unprecedented lengths to build hotels, the landmark Tower of the Americas, pavilions, and a convention center to stage HemisFair '68. HemisFair Arena also was built for the fair, later giving the city a home for the American Basketball Association's Dallas Chaparrals, which arrived in 1973 and would soon become the San Antonio Spurs. The six-month celebration elevated San Antonio's stature throughout the hemisphere, particularly in neighboring Mexico. More and more people from all points of the compass were finding San Antonio and its newly commercialized River Walk a great place to visit. HemisFair '68 resulted in the construction of the city's convention center and the Hilton Palacio del Rio convention hotel, and it launched many locally owned businesses that prospered and became central to San Antonio's economy and employment base. It did not create greater opportunities for communities of color. That would soon change in ways the Anglo establishment figures of the day could have never imagined or anticipated.

Building on the post-Depression work of grassroots community organizer Saul Alinsky in Chicago, one of his acolytes, Ernesto "Ernie" Cortez, returned to San Antonio to form the nonpartisan Communities Organized for Public Service (COPS) in 1974. While some might describe COPS as a civil rights group, that would be selling it short. Its core aim was to pressure the powers-to-be to end discriminatory practices, including the inequitable distribution of public resources. Mexican Americans demanded to be treated equitably. Cortez enlisted like-minded Catholic parish priests on the city's West Side and South Side and empowered women for the first time to join in the work. COPS used a variety of nonviolent protest tactics to bring municipal and business leaders to the table, and the outcome over the ensuing decades has been transformative. More than $1 billion in public investment in the inner city has been recorded in the fifty years of COPS's presence in San Antonio.

The Good Government League had long controlled political offices in San Antonio, even if many of its wealthier members lived in adjacent municipalities like Alamo Heights, Olmos Park, and Terrell Hills, where even elite Mexican Americans and Blacks felt unwelcome. Those ruling elites could not vote in San Antonio's city elections, but that didn't stop them from exerting control over every aspect of public life. Meanwhile, the same elites lived in the near–North Side municipalities with their own mayors and city councils, police forces, and school districts as well as private schools and exclusionary social clubs. The success of COPS, various civil rights organizations, and groups like the Southwest Voter Registration Education Project (SVREP) brought more Mexican American citizens to the polls. It was only a matter of time before the institutions and a coterie of wealthy families would find their control of San Antonio's government shared with leaders from the city's poorest neighborhoods and parishes.

Facing pressure from within as well as the federal courts, San Antonio in 1977 reorganized itself politically after a close and contentious election resulted in the formation of single-member districts, finally abandoning at-large elections and the backroom selection of candidates by the ruling elites. Various rounds of public planning programs resulted in more equitable systems of distributing goods and services. Inner-city neighborhood infrastructure improved incrementally, especially storm drainage and street maintenance.

The ten-member city council, elected in single-member district elections, began to resemble the city's general population, although the city charter still made members' service voluntary. The mayor received a token fifty-dollar stipend for each council meeting, while council members received twenty dollars. That would not change until 2010.

A decade earlier, San Antonio benefited greatly from the 1968 arrival of Brig. Gen. (ret.) Robert P. McDermott, a former commandant of the Air Force Academy hired to serve as CEO of the United Services Automobile Association (USAA), the fast-growing insurance giant with corporate headquarters originally located on Broadway and later housed in a giant development in northwest San Antonio that resembles the Pentagon. "McD," as he was universally known, was more than a retired general and business leader. He was a leading civic evangelist for change and growth. The Boston native also was far more receptive to Latino participation in power sharing than some of the homegrown Anglo leadership. He proved pivotal in uniting other forward-thinking business leaders, particularly in the realm of economic development with the founding of the San Antonio Economic Development Foundation, now known as greater:SATX.

One way San Antonians from all parts of the city and from all points on the economic spectrum come together is Fiesta, a celebration born in the late nineteenth century that celebrates Texas independence and, in its early decades by default, Anglo domination of San Antonio's historical narrative. By the 1980s and '90s, it was steadily evolving, again under growing pressure from representative groups, to make room for all segments of the community to celebrate. The Fiesta Commission began to recognize an ever-expanding festival of parades, parties, and the crowning of faux kings, queens, duchesses, and their courtesans. Countless social events are staged now throughout the city. This complex mix of cultures, peoples, and traditions underscores the city's historical differences even as the April festival celebrates the city's confluence of peoples.

In the 1980s, San Antonio forged a nascent trade and commercial relationship with Japan. At the same time, Mexico opened its economy, setting the stage for the North American Free Trade Agreement (NAFTA), which quickly generated increased truck and rail freight traffic between Mexico and the United States, especially along I-35, which reaches from Laredo on the border and extends beyond Texas north to the Canadian border.

The Mexican tradition Día de los Muertos, or Day of the Dead, is celebrated with a Fiesta parade in San Antonio. Photo by Al Rendon.

One year after NAFTA was initialed by the three nations' elected leaders in San Antonio in 1992, the city opened the sixty-five-thousand-seat Alamodome, built on a former East Side industrial site. The Alamodome debuted with the staging of the 1993 US Olympic Festival. Since then, the dome has hosted multiple National Collegiate Athletic Association Men's and Women's Regional and Final Four tournaments, annual Alamo Bowl college football games, many rock concerts, convention meetings, entertainment events, and high school and college graduations. For some years, it was home to the Spurs, including the team's first National Basketball Association championship in 1999. San Antonio, however, has been frustrated in its various attempts to attract a National Football League franchise or expansion team, a subject covered in greater depth in chapter 11. The election that narrowly approved the construction of the Alamodome left opponents bitter in defeat, but over its three decades, the multipurpose domed facility has generated $4 billion in economic impact. Years later, in 2003, an overwhelming majority of voters would approve Bexar County's construction of a new arena for the Spurs. For more than two decades, it was known as the SBC Center, then the AT&T Center. It was renamed the Frost Bank Center in 2023.

The collapse of the Soviet Union and an end to the Cold War would eventually be felt in San Antonio and in other US cities and communities with military installations. With the decline in congressional funding for the military, Pentagon officials looked to economize on base expenditures to free up funds for continuing technology advances in weaponry, intelligence gathering, and projecting US military power abroad. Base closures and consolidated missions became the order of the day. The Base Realignment and Closure Commission (BRAC) formed by the Pentagon spared San Antonio's military installations in its 1988, 1991, and 1993 rounds of cuts, but local officials could see the inevitable coming, and in 1995, the decision to close Kelly AFB, a major logistics and supply deposit and training facility, was announced. Once home to more than twenty thousand civilian workers, Kelly closed for good in 2001, its closure slowed by the efforts of local officials to buy time to absorb the job losses. Soon after, BRAC announced the closure of Brooks AFB, home to aerospace medicine.

City leaders faced serious challenges in those years: how to diversify an economy overly dependent on civilian employment at local military installations and on the convention-and-visitor industry, which generated mostly low-wage service and hospitality industry jobs. Amid growing cross-border trade and investments, it was Japan that brought an entire new economic sector to San Antonio: automotive and advanced manufacturing. Japan's Toyota Motor Corp. in 2003 announced its selection of San Antonio for a world-class assembly plant to be built on the city's economically depressed South Side. In 2006, Toyota pickup trucks began rolling off the line, eventually reaching 240,000 vehicles produced annually. The factory campus includes more than twenty on-site suppliers. Toyota Texas and its integrated network of suppliers employ about 8,200 people, according to the company's website, who today produce both gas-driven and hybrid Tundras and Sequoia SUVs. The strategically located factory serves as a link along the automotive corridor that stretches from Detroit to the

US South, with a growing number of assembly plants and steel parts makers in northern Mexico.

San Antonio today is a key link to the automotive industry's North American supply chain, even more so now with other manufacturers establishing operations here. Those include Navistar Inc.'s heavy-truck plant and British rolling-stock manufacturer JCB's announcement in 2023 that it would build its second North American factory on San Antonio's South Side. Continental North America opened a new manufacturing facility in New Braunfels in 2022 to produce advanced driver assistance systems and eventually will employ five hundred workers in addition to the more than three hundred workers employed at the company's vehicle powertrain plant in Seguin. Tesla has built vehicle manufacturing and battery production plants near Austin and Corpus Christi and announced plans to build a vehicle manufacturing plant in Monterrey, Mexico. Some of its suppliers are establishing a base in San Antonio. In all, Elon Musk's companies—Tesla, SpaceX, and Boring Co.—have purchased 346 parcels of Texas land in a five-year period, according to media reports. The appraised value of those purchases at last report totaled more than $2.5 billion. Much of that land is in Central Texas, near the GigaTexas factory now operating in Southeast Austin. Support sites include Hutto, Kyle, and San Antonio, according to CoStar News, adding more than fifteen thousand advanced manufacturing jobs to Central Texas.

Over time, San Antonio's two shuttered military bases became home to two very different types of developments. Kelly became Port San Antonio, a 1,900-acre technology and innovation hub with a focus on aerospace, defense, global logistics, advanced manufacturing, cybersecurity, and education, together employing more than 18,000 people and generating $6.5 billion in annual economic activity, exceeding the impact of the former logistics base. When the decision was made in 1995 to close Kelly AFB, the installation workforce had been downsized to 14,000 civilian workers, but the annual economic impact was still estimated to be $4.3 billion. Port San Antonio's proximity and shared airfield with Lackland AFB helped inform its evolution. Brooks AFB, on San Antonio's Southeast Side, became Brooks, an economic development hub with multifamily, commercial, and retail tenants. The former 1,308-acre base now includes a major pharmaceutical manufacturer, the University of Incarnate Word School of Osteopathic Medicine, and a growing job base that today employs 5,300 and a residential population of 1,700 people.

Military intelligence agencies operating in San Antonio began phasing in new systems in the post–Cold War era. As personnel were discharged from active military activity, they became entrepreneurial and formed network security companies in San Antonio. Today, San Antonio has the second-highest count of cybersecurity companies outside of Washington, DC, and the largest campus of the National Security Agency outside Fort Meade, Maryland. The changing nature of warfare and the city's open doors to the US military have led to new, still-developing elements in San Antonio's increasingly diversified economy. Drone pilots now train at Randolph Air Force Base.

Austin is far better known as a national tech hub, but San Antonio's rapid growth in aerospace and twenty-first-century defense and cybersecurity and its growing advanced manufacturing base are well-kept secrets even among many San Antonians. That same could be said for the Southwest Research Institute, an applied research center located on a former 1,200-acre cattle ranch in northwest San Antonio, and the adjacent Texas Biomedical Research Institute, which specializes in infectious disease research. Organizations like the nonprofit Tech Bloc have helped fuel awareness of San Antonio's tech community and given it a greater voice at city hall. Geekdom—a start-up incubator and coworking space, the creation of downtown real estate developer Graham Weston—has launched dozens of companies that together have attracted hundreds of millions of dollars in investment capital and purchase agreements. Many were started by former employees of Rackspace, the hosting and cloud computing company Weston cofounded in the late 1990s. In 2022, Geekdom had 104 start-ups operating in its ecosystem, a sign of growing entrepreneurial activity in San Antonio. According to the latest estimate in 2022, San Antonio's information technology sector had an economic impact of almost $11 billion, triple its size in 2000.

Rapid population growth, the emergence of the University of Texas at San Antonio (UTSA) as a Tier One research university, improved education and workforce development outcomes, and a municipal push to develop more affordable housing are combining to make San Antonio a city that more and more people want to call home. How fast is San Antonio growing? San Antonio led all US cities in numerical growth from 2016 to 2017, from 2020 to 2021, and for the third time, between 2022 and 2023, with a gain in that twelve-month period of 21,970 people within city limits. Between 2022 and 2023, the San Antonio–New Braunfels metro area grew by 48,071 people, according to the US Census, or 132 people per day over the twelve-month period, to push the metro's population to 2.7 million. During the same period, Bexar County placed eighth in the nation in growth among US counties, with a one-year gain of 27,488 people.

San Antonio's top employers lead the charge for the city's high-ranking population growth. The US Department of Defense's Joint Base San Antonio (JBSA), comprising Lackland, Fort Sam Houston, and Randolph installations and their training units, employs an estimated 60,000 people, while military spending has an annual economic impact of $39 billion. JBSA is now the single largest unified military base in the country. Lackland remains the US Air Force's basic training installation and home to the Twenty-Fourth Air Force, a critical cyber warfare defense command. Randolph is a leading pilot training installation and home to the Air Education and Training Command, while BAMC at JBSA–Fort Sam Houston now ranks as the world's largest medical school. Today, it provides medical training for all the US military's branches. BAMC not only provides care for wounded US military troops; it also offers health-care services to San Antonio residents. From 2000 to 2020, San Antonio had more than 2,650 firms with military contracts totaling more than $55.42 billion.

San Antonio's largest private employers are diversified (see table 3.1).

Health care and biosciences are now the largest employment sector in San Antonio, employing one in six San Antonio workers, adding up to 160,000 jobs and a $44 billion economic impact in

Table 3.1.

San Antonio area's top private employers, approximate jobs

Employer	Approximate jobs
H-E-B grocery chain	20,000
USAA	19,000
UT Health San Antonio	7,930
Rackspace	6,300
Whataburger	6,000
Rush Enterprises	5,000

Source: greater:SATX.

2019. Researchers at UT Health San Antonio, with its medical and dental schools, had 740 clinical trials underway in 2022, one-third of which were focused on new cancer treatments. UT Health is scheduled to be merged into the larger UTSA in 2025.

Conventions and tourism, while not yet back to prepandemic levels, remain important pillars in San Antonio's economy, with 140,000 workers and a $15.2 billion economic impact in 2023. Tourism taxes paid to the city that year totaled $229 million. Tourism numbers in 2020 and 2021 were set back because of the COVID-19 pandemic, largely from the cancellations of conventions, and have yet to recover fully. Yet multiple new hotels continue to be developed in the urban core. Among five hotels under construction in 2024, at least another 1,371 rooms were planned. The city attracts about thirty-four million visitors annually, according to Visit San Antonio. The Henry B. González Convention Center, greatly expanded in 2017, is set to expand again as part of a proposal to enhance the Alamodome and create a downtown sports district.

The city's higher education institutions produce more than 32,300 graduates annually. UTSA, with its first graduating class in 1976, is still considered young. Yet UTSA's main campus in northwest San Antonio and its rapidly expanding downtown campus serve 34,742 undergraduates, 4,662 graduate students, and almost 1,000 doctoral students. Texas A&M University–San Antonio is even younger, founded in 2009 and now serving 7,400 students on the city's South Side. San Antonio is the only Texas city with branch universities of the state's top two higher education systems.

UTSA has evolved from a commuter school to one offering advanced degrees in engineering, data science, and soon, artificial intelligence, among other science, technology, engineering, and mathematics focuses. Its Small Business Development Center is a model for similar programs throughout the Caribbean and Latin America. The institute sparks almost $3 billion in economic impact locally and nationally.

Another milestone occurred in 2010 when Lloyd Potter was approved by the Texas governor to become the Texas state demographer, an action that also moved the Texas Demographic Center (TDC) to UTSA. The TDC operates as part of the US Census Bureau and offers advanced degrees. It predicts population growth for the state's 254 counties through 2060, a vital planning tool for determining infrastructure needs.

Private universities have long histories in San Antonio, including Trinity University and the three Catholic institutions, St. Mary's University, Incarnate Word University, and Our Lady of the Lake University. The Alamo District's community college system had a 2022 enrollment of 66,000 students. Altogether, 130,000 students attend higher education institutions in the city. The Alamo Promise program is enabling many of those students to attend tuition-free and then move on to seek a four-year degree at UTSA or A&M–San Antonio in an extension of the program.

The cost of living in San Antonio is rising, but housing and other costs remained well below the national average in 2021. That is no comfort for the city's many low-wage earners. Half of the families and individuals renting housing are paying more than 30 percent of their income for housing, which experts consider a formula for financial trouble. Nearly 100,000 families are on a waiting list for subsidized housing or housing vouchers, while the city has a shortfall of at least 150,000 affordable housing units. Like Austin, San Antonio's inadequate number of available rental units has caused rents to spike in recent years, and San Antonio is attracting new residents at a far greater rate than it is adding new homes and apartments, a crisis explored more deeply in chapter 9.

San Antonio, like Austin, remains a population magnet, even as it faces significant infrastructure challenges. That growth continues to expand the city's tax bases and to keep local government on sound fiscal footing. Continued robust growth is certain in the years ahead. Austin is growing fast. San Antonio is growing fast. The two cities are growing together fast.

Fast-Growing Cities and Counties Redefine the Austin–San Antonio Corridor

I think the growth in our community means that more people are coming here looking for quality of life.
—Former New Braunfels Mayor Rusty Brockman

Life is good in the many growing cities and communities within commuting distance of the core cities of Austin and San Antonio, the bookend metros that anchor multiple municipalities. Some of these smaller cities make the list of the nation's fastest-growing cities. Families seeking more affordable housing, lower crime rates, strong public school districts, and in many instances, a small-town culture are fueling dramatic growth in what demographers once called "bedroom communities." Today, Georgetown, Round Rock, Kyle, San Marcos, New Braunfels, Seguin, Boerne, and Floresville, among others, are fast-growing, freestanding cities with their own distinct identities and attractions.

An emerging trend among these cities is the phenomenon of families with two working professionals, one employed in Austin or San Antonio, the other in another city in the region. Various communities are competing to attract these dual-city commuters. In some instances, one spouse heads north to Austin for work, while the other heads south to San Antonio. More and more

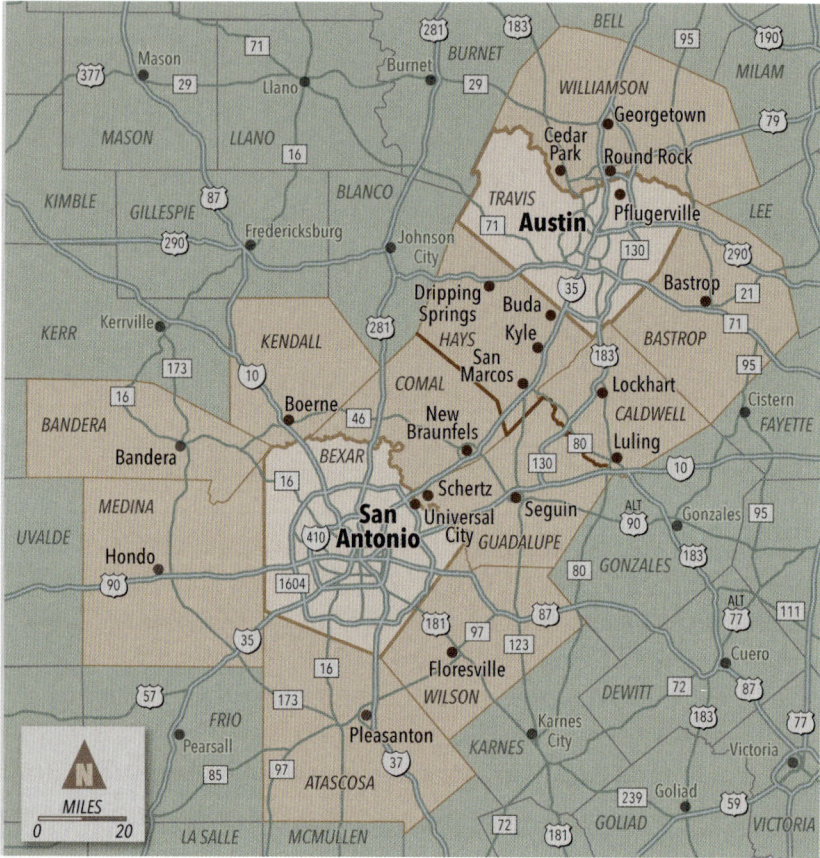

The thirteen counties of the Austin–San Antonio metropolitan statistical area: Atascosa, Bandera, Bastrop, Bexar, Caldwell, Comal, Guadalupe, Hays, Kendall, Medina, Travis, Williamson, and Wilson. Map by Mike Fisher.

workers, US Census data show, are working remotely and can live anywhere with reliable broadband service. Many more are working a hybrid schedule, reducing the number of days spent commuting from home to office. This poses a challenge for downtown office tower landlords. The postpandemic migration of workers and their families is evident throughout the Texas Triangle cities of Dallas–Fort Worth, Houston, and Austin–San Antonio, though the trend is still evolving. Reliable data are probably several years in the future. The smaller size of these corridor cities disguises their extraordinary rate of growth, not unlike what demographers saw in the Mid-Cities between Dallas and Fort Worth in the 1970s and 1980s.

The big-city growth around Travis and Bexar Counties is most notable in Hays, Comal, and Williamson Counties (see table 4.1), followed by growth to the west in Kendall County and to the east in Guadalupe County.

Hays County, with San Marcos as its county seat, was the single fastest-growing US county between 2010 and 2020, with a nearly 53 percent increase in population. Its neighbor to the south, Comal County, which includes New Braunfels, was the second fastest-growing county nationwide, with a 50.8 percent increase over the same decade. There are 254 counties in Texas, and there are 3,143 counties nationally. The two fastest-growing counties nationally are in the Austin–San Antonio corridor.

Of the top fifteen fastest-growing cities, four are in the Austin–San Antonio region (see table 4.2).

The cities along I-35, especially San Marcos in Hays County and New Braunfels in Comal County, represent the area where the Austin and San Antonio metros have merged more than anywhere else in the thirteen-county megaregion. Newer residential, commercial, and industrial sites have left no discernible bands of vacant land along I-35 that could keep Austin's urban sphere separate from San Antonio's. It is as if Austin and San Antonio are joined at the hip at the Hays and Comal County borders. But

Table 4.1.

Austin–San Antonio metro counties top ten nationally in growth, 2010–2020

National ranking	County	Growth
No. 1	Hays (San Marcos)	52.7%
No. 2	Comal (New Braunfels)	50.8%
No. 6	Williamson (Georgetown)	44.8%

Source: US Census Bureau.

Table 4.2.

Austin–San Antonio corridor cities with more than fifty thousand
population and their one-year growth rate, 2021–2022

Corridor city	National ranking	One-year growth rate
Georgetown	No. 1	14.4%
Kyle	No. 3	10.9%
Leander	No. 4	10.9%
New Braunfels	No. 13	5.7%

Source: US Census Bureau and author calculations.

substantial urban growth has occurred north of Austin and south
of San Antonio, notably in Round Rock and Georgetown, north of
Austin, and Floresville, south of San Antonio.

San Marcos and New Braunfels

Understanding how Austin and San Antonio have grown in connectivity is most visible in the Hays and Comal corridor counties,
anchored by the cities of San Marcos and New Braunfels, respectively. Industrial parks located alongside I-35 have generated many
of the jobs attracting people moving to those counties. There is
much more to those cities than industrial parks.

"I think the growth in our community means that more people are coming here looking for quality of life," said former New
Braunfels Mayor Rusty Brockman. "What our chamber and city
have done really well over the years is to recruit really good-paying
jobs, good businesses, technology-related businesses, and tier-one
automotive suppliers."

Being near San Antonio has helped New Braunfels. "We touted
our workforce," Brockman said. "We are in between two metropolitan areas. Our neighbor to the south, San Antonio, brings so
much to the entire region. We want to be partners. I think it has
become one of those opportunities that we had taken for granted
that we were close to an international airport. We were close to

commerce and trade. Our workforce is shared with San Antonio.... We've patterned around what San Antonio has done."

New Braunfels and Comal County offer job-training programs that aim to attract continued business investment there. "I see a well-trained workforce that is going to be trained right here because we have the Alamo Colleges here. We have Texas State Technical College here and our Central Texas Technology Center. What I see are students graduating from our high schools and not necessarily leaving town. They can drive to San Marcos and San Antonio for jobs," Brockman said. "By 2032, it appears we will be built out within the city limits. What we are planning now ... somewhere along the line, we are going to need to go upward downtown and along I-35, even as we work to protect our history."

New Braunfels's population crossed the 100,000 threshold around 2022, reaching 104,707. Brockman projects continuing growth, eventually reaching 200,000 people.

Shoppers browse at the large New Braunfels Buc-ee's store for snacks, drinks, and nonfood products. The Buc-ee's chain, known for clean restrooms and numerous gasoline pumps, operates two stores in the Austin–San Antonio area, one in New Braunfels and another in Luling, near Seguin. A third Buc-ee's store is planned near Boerne. Photo by Benjamin Charles.

"New Braunfels is one of the special towns in Texas," observed San Antonio business leader Graham Weston, a cofounder of the cloud computing giant Rackspace who grew up on a ranch between Marion and New Braunfels. "I think you will see more high-rises, more density."

Part of the allure of New Braunfels, even as it grows rapidly, is the city's German heritage, which dates to the settlement founded in 1845 by Prince Carl of Solms-Braunfels in Germany. He led hundreds of Germans immigrating to Texas through the port of Galveston to the two leagues (8,856.8 acres) of land he purchased for a little more than $1,000, land that included Guadalupe River frontage and Comal Springs.

Thousands more Germans followed, eventually establishing other settlements in the Texas Hill Country, notably Fredericksburg, Comfort, and Boerne. Many German families later found their way to San Antonio. New Braunfels retains its historic downtown but is otherwise growing with new subdivision homes selling as fast as developers can convert former ranches and farmland into new suburbs.

New Braunfels is the headquarters of the publicly traded Rush Enterprises, the largest dealership network of commercial vehicles in the nation. Continental Automotive started a manufacturing site in New Braunfels in 2022 making equipment for vehicles with assisted and automated driving. Companies building housing in the New Braunfels area include SouthStar Communities, Bainbridge Companies, MNO Partners, and Tricon Residential, as well as developer Will Korioth. Schlitterbahn Waterpark is another long-established employer and summer tourist attraction.

San Marcos, twenty miles to the northeast along the corridor, is part of the Austin metropolitan statistical area. There is no mistaking the I-35 commuter's arrival in San Marcos. That stretch of the interstate highway is home to the San Marcos Outlet Malls, which actually are two distinct malls, the San Marcos Premium Outlets and the Tanger Factory Outlet Center. Together, the malls offer shoppers 240 stores occupying more than one million square feet of retail shopping. While the discount outlets of leading retail brands are a major attraction for regional shoppers, San Marcos is best known as the home of Texas State University, the city's biggest employer. Founded in 1899, its campus landmarks are visible high on hills shaded by mature oaks. Texas State has grown to serve more than thirty-eight thousand undergraduate and graduate students, making it the seventh-largest public university in the state, and as the school's website notes, it is "the only Texas university to graduate a U.S. president." The school was known as Southwest Texas State Teachers College in 1930, the year Lyndon B. Johnson graduated with a history degree and teacher certificate. In fact, the university has had eight different names over its 124-year history, finally gaining its present name of Texas State University in 2013.

While New Braunfels has Comal Springs and the popular Schlitterbahn Waterpark, San Marcos has the San Marcos River and Springs, which have never run dry. From 1950 to 1996, San Marcos was home to another popular tourist attraction, Aquarena Springs, with its underwater fiberglass volcano, performing mermaids, and more. The river is still home to a Texas State tradition: Graduating bobcats celebrate by jumping into the river still wearing caps and gowns.

The two springs have attracted people for thousands of years. Archaeologists have dated prehistoric campsites and artifacts found at the springs to the Clovis period, twelve thousand years ago, making it one of the oldest such sites in the Southwest. "Because of the springs, archaeologists tell us we are the longest continuously inhabited location in North America. We're proud of that. We have beautiful hill country," San Marcos Mayor Jane Hughson said.

San Marcos dates its founding to about the same time New Braunfels was established. While a very early nineteenth-century settlement established by Spanish families who arrived from New Spain did not survive, Anglo settlers arrived in 1846, and two years later, the Texas Legislature recognized San Marcos as the seat of Hays County.

Both New Braunfels and San Marcos served for more than a century as regional centers supporting local economies built around agriculture, mostly cotton production and cattle ranching. The arrival of the railroad around 1880 helped family businesses expand to serve new markets and enjoy new levels of prosperity.

Not many people today are aware that San Marcos was home to a World War II Army Air Corps navigator training base established in 1942. More than ten thousand navigators were trained at San Marcos Army Airfield before the war ended. The base was then slated for closure, but US Rep. Lyndon B. Johnson successfully intervened to keep it open through the Korean War as a helicopter pilot training base. The base was renamed Gary Air Force Base in honor of 2nd Lt. Arthur Edward Gary, who died when Japanese bombers attacked Clark Field in the Philippines on December 7, 1941, making him the first San Marcos resident killed in World War II. The base was closed in 1963. Today, the San Marcos Airport and a job-training center are on the site of the former military airfield.

Elsewhere in Hays County, out-of-state companies, including Walton Global Holdings LLC of Arizona and Majestic Realty Co. of Southern California, are investing heavily. Majestic has plans for up to two million square feet of space for mixed development speculative space. Walton plans to spend $103 million over the next decade to construct additional industrial buildings.

"We have new subdivisions on the north end of town and the south end of town," said Mayor Hughson. "We have two Amazon fulfillment centers and the Hill Country Studios. To the north and south, our ETJ [extraterritorial jurisdiction] meets up with Kyle and New Braunfels. To the west, we discourage dense development because that is where the Edwards Aquifer recharge zone and contributing zone are. So we have limits on that side, but on the east side, that's where our growth is going."

San Marcos is planning for continuing residential growth. "I think our housing will become more dense. We did change our land development code to allow for smaller lots. That has helped us get more housing into the same amount of space. A lot of people like less yards. Houses are selling very quickly," explained Hughson, a committee member of the Austin–San Antonio Corridor Council and a former chairwoman for the Capital Area Council of Governments.

Housing in both cities is still affordable by national standards, but Texans accustomed to prices far below the cost of living in the state's urban centers are encountering rising housing costs throughout the corridor. "It's been a problem we've been dealing with for about five years. We see people who work here, but they can't live here, and they live somewhere else and are driving to work," Brockman said.

Closer to Austin on the I-35 corridor, Buda and Kyle, both in Hays County, were until recently small towns between Austin and San Marcos. Both are expanding rapidly with housing and commercial developments as more workers in Austin seek affordable housing within commuting distance of the capital. Tesla's Giga-Texas factory, for example, is about a thirty-minute commute from the two smaller cities via the lightly trafficked SH 130 toll road. Tesla also has leased one million square feet of space in Kyle, where five Tesla suppliers have located. "Our goal is to be, quite simply, the employment center of choice in this region," said Kyle City Manager Brian Langley at the 2023 State of the City address. "We want to have a great culture, great pay, great benefits, and most importantly, a great community. We believe we're well on our way to doing all [of] those things."

As the city grows and its staff expands to increase its economic development potential, Kyle also is working to expand in ways that make the community more livable. An eight-mile, east-west Plum Creek Trail for walking and cycling has been built and likely will be lengthened.

In 2023 and 2024, Kyle's residential growth was so strong, it ran short on water. San Marcos City Council voted in both years to sell up to more than one hundred million gallons of Edwards Aquifer water rights to its nearby neighbor in a contract that expired at the end of 2024. The sale stands as an example of how regional communities are willing to assist one another through rough periods, the type of cooperation that boosts the entire megaregion.

According to US Census Bureau data, Kyle's population grew 85 percent between 2010 and 2021 to 51,789. In the same period, Buda's population rose by 114 percent to 15,643.

Kyle and Buda's proximity to the Tesla Inc. pickup truck plant makes both cities popular places to live, with housing costs far more affordable than in Travis County. Residents who work outside Austin also avoid traffic congestion closer to downtown Austin.

But don't call Kyle a "bedroom community," at least not around Mayor Travis Mitchell.

"If we don't have our eyes very focused on what we are trying to achieve as a city, I think it's possible for the market to sort of pigeonhole the city of Kyle into being just a bedroom community or maybe a very large bedroom community," Mitchell said at his 2023 State of the City address. He continued,

> That has never been my vision, has never been the vision of the city. What we want to do is create a thriving, robust, balanced economy in our city for folks who work here and earn primary jobs where they can have breakfast, lunch, and dinner options. And they can have fitness classes and yoga classes and opportunities to volunteer at their PTA or with a school district. Those are the things that we care about a lot . . . a harmony between the external forces that are trying to make an impact on our community and the internal forces, our own community itself and the leadership who are trying to harness that and shape something meaningful.

The affluent rural town of Dripping Springs in western Hays County is another population magnet. Between 2010 and 2021, it grew by 224 percent to 5,787 people, resulting in some home prices surpassing $900,000. The quaint Hill Country town is known as a backdrop for numerous feature films and television series. Dripping Springs markets itself as the "Gateway to the Hill Country." One of its biggest businesses is hosting wedding celebrations.

Lockhart, eighteen miles east of San Marcos, calls itself the "Barbecue Capital of Texas" and is popular for its much-trafficked, antique-laden central business district. It has become something of a refuge for longtime Austinites priced out of the market. As Caldwell County's seat, Lockhart's 2021 population estimate of 14,844 was 16 percent higher than in 2010. Planned housing development on Lockhart's outskirts will carry the population number higher in the next few years.

Nearby to Lockhart, Bastrop, with a population of 11,679, was named in 2024 by billionaire Elon Musk as the new headquarters for his social media giant X, previously known as Twitter. This is among other Musk investments in the Bastrop area, along with his electric-vehicle Tesla plant in east Travis County.

Schertz, Cibolo, Selma, and Live Oak

San Antonio includes a network of growing cities in its five-county metro region. Along I-35 between San Antonio and New Braunfels are the fast-growing suburbs of Schertz, Cibolo, and Selma, which have teamed up to expand business development through a single chamber of commerce. Schertz, whose city limits cross into Bexar, Guadalupe, and Comal Counties, grew by 23 percent between 2010 and 2022 to 43,010. It is home to the state's largest Amazon fulfillment center, one of the company's most extensive at more than one million square feet.

Cibolo, in Guadalupe County, is smaller than Schertz, with a population of 34,814, but if the 118 percent growth it has realized from 2010 to 2022 continues, it likely will catch up in the future. "People move here for that hometown feel but with the closeness to big-city amenities like our retail and restaurants," said Cibolo Public Relations Manager Christine Pollock. "We still maintain that small-town charm where you can walk down the street and see your neighbors." Cibolo's population in 2000 was 5,000, yet a strong tax base driven by growth in single-family homes has kept the historic central business district thriving. Now, as the city grows, local leaders are making plans to build a convention center and attract the city's first major hotel.

Selma was founded in 1849 by German settlers as a stagecoach stop along the Old Austin Road, now the path of I-35. Like Schertz, its city limits reach into Bexar, Comal, and Guadalupe Counties. Its location sixteen miles northeast of San Antonio has transformed the small community of 17,023 into a thriving suburb. Most metro residents know Selma as home to the Retama Race Track, which, along with the city's history as a stagecoach stop, accounts for the horse head found in the city's logo.

Live Oak, just north of Selma, population 15,993, is growing more slowly, but the arrival in 2019 of the Scandinavian IKEA store, which specializes in ready-to-assemble furniture, textiles, lighting, and home decor, has introduced tens of thousands of shoppers to the city.

Georgetown and Round Rock

Georgetown and Round Rock are examples of fast-growing towns north of Austin and on the opposite side of Austin from the San Antonio metro. While Georgetown and Round Rock are not part of the area where the two metros merge, they contribute significantly to the growing profile of the megaregion.

Georgetown, founded in 1848, is the seat of Williamson County, where residential growth is exploding north of Austin. Forests for wood building, good water, and fertile ground were the early magnets of the first settlers who arrived from numerous states and European nations.

The opening of Southwestern University in 1873 and a rail line five years later expanded the appeal. Georgetown sat along a well-used cattle trail, too, which fed into the Kansas-bound trails that included the Chisholm and the Dodge City. The creation of a flood-control dam that became Lake Georgetown drew people for employment in manufacturing and quarry operations. Cotton farms surrounded the town.

Multiple factors are responsible for Georgetown's rapid growth in population in recent decades, in addition to its lake and university. One, of course, is the route of I-35 and its attendant flow of commerce and people. Job creation in Austin and at the Dell campus in Round Rock, thirteen miles to the south, accounts for significant growth. The other is the way the city has preserved its historic character with a Main Street program that spawned the restoration of 1800s buildings and houses.

"Job growth in Georgetown and across the Austin metro continues to bring new residents to our city," Mayor Josh Schroeder said. "People are moving here for the same reasons that brought many of us to Georgetown—wonderful and safe neighborhoods, fantastic parks and events, and welcoming people. We continue

Dell Technologies Inc.'s headquarters are in Round Rock. Photo by Jjpwiki (Wikimedia Commons, CC BY-SA 4.0).

to adjust our plans and build new infrastructure to maintain the great quality of life for all of us who are proud to call Georgetown our home."

Georgetown was a sleepier community in 1980 with a population of 9,468; by 2020, that number had grown a remarkable sevenfold to 67,176. By 2022, it had reached 86,507. At its present rate, the city will surpass 100,000 residents by 2025. Georgetown gained notice as the country's fastest-growing city by percentage of population in the United States in both 2016 and 2022 among cities with more than 50,000 residents and made the top ten list every year from 2015 to the present. From 2021 to 2022, the city grew at a stunning rate of 14.4 percent. Williamson County was the tenth-fastest-growing county between 2022 and 2023, according to the US Census, with a 24,918 population gain. This growth comes with challenges. Georgetown's current water supply will become insufficient by 2030, according to the *San Antonio Express-News*. By 2070, Georgetown projects it will need an additional ninety-nine-thousand-acre-foot supply, possibly from groundwater.

Round Rock, closer to Austin than Georgetown, was founded in 1854 along Brushy Creek. The name stems from a distinctive limestone outcropping along the creek. The same rail line that passed through Georgetown also served tiny Round Rock. Locals used the rail to deliver products from a broom factory and a lime plant. Round Rock, like Georgetown, preserved its 1800s-era buildings in a central square called Old Town. Round Rock grew modestly across the decades from the 1900s until the 1980s; no one could have anticipated what would happen in short order after that as Austin's growth spilled northward. Round Rock, after all, is only sixteen miles north of downtown Austin along I-35.

Something more significant was underfoot. A University of Texas at Austin freshman began selling simple computers and parts out of his dorm room and car trunk. His name is Michael Dell, and the story of what would become Dell Technologies has become Texas and global business lore. Dell's company expanded in offices and manufacturing facilities in Austin and was soon on its way to making acquisitions of other companies to become a world-leading computer hardware company. The phenomenal growth of the company and the prosperity of many of its employees who acquired wealth through stock options even led to a new term in Austin for those tech workers: Dellionaires.

In 1996, Dell Inc. started the move of its headquarters to Round Rock, where it remains today. About 14,000 of the company's 165,000 global workers are employed in the Austin metro area. Only three years after moving to Round Rock, the company's sales tax receipts funded nearly half of the City of Round Rock's general fund. In 2023, Dell Technologies ranked thirty-fourth in revenues on *Fortune* magazine's 500 list, one of three companies on the list with headquarters in the Austin metro area, along with electric vehicle–maker Tesla and software giant Oracle. In fiscal year 2022, Dell Technologies reported $101.6 billion in revenues.

Nearby Dell headquarters in Round Rock is Dell Diamond, a minor-league baseball stadium seating 11,631, which opened in 2000. The Triple-A Round Rock Express team is affiliated with the

Texas Rangers. Round Rock and Georgetown share Nolan Ryan, the retired Major League Baseball Hall of Fame right-handed pitcher. "I live in Georgetown and work in Round Rock," said Ryan, a co-owner of the Round Rock Express and the Double-A San Antonio Missions. Ryan's business offices are on the second floor of a bank building next door to the ballpark. Thanks to Dell and its proximity to Austin, Round Rock's population skyrocketed to 126,697 in 2022, making it the third-largest municipality in the Austin–San Antonio region.

Seguin, Boerne, and Floresville

Seguin, the seat of Guadalupe County, sits on the banks of the Guadalupe River near the junction of I-10 and SH 130, a lightly trafficked toll road built to relieve I-35 congestion, thirty miles to the east of San Antonio and sixty miles south of Austin. Named after Texas revolutionary hero Col. Juan Seguin, mayor of San Antonio at the time of the 1836 Battle of the Alamo, and founded in 1838, Seguin is one of the state's fastest-growing cities. Its population grew from 22,011 in 2000 to 33,408 in 2022. Seguin is home to the small liberal arts and faith-based Texas Lutheran University, but its economy is driven by manufacturing, a sector that has grown robustly in recent years.

Seguin, home to a large Caterpillar heavy-equipment plant, is absorbing new growth from the $75 million construction of the Maruichi Stainless Tube Corp. plant making tubes for the semiconductor industry and from an $18 million expansion by United Alloy of a plant making sheet metal and powder coatings. As in Comal County, Walton Global Holdings has acquired acreage for new housing to accommodate expected population growth.

In 2024, the City of Seguin and the Seguin Economic Development Corp. wrote the city's first comprehensive economic development strategy. The plan targets industries and lists infrastructure needs to stay on a growth path driven by the expansion of the movement of people and goods along SH 130, the parallel alternative to I-35.

Boerne, the Kendall County seat incorporated in 1909, is located northwest of San Antonio along I-10, its population growing from 6,178 in 2000 to 20,707 in 2022. Median household income is around $80,000, significantly higher than in San Antonio. By preserving its bustling Main Street, period architecture, and the community's German culture, Boerne has burnished its distinct character and become a regional visitor draw. Its scenic setting in the Hill Country, excellent schools, and small-town feel distinguish it from other cities located on the outskirts of San Antonio. Attractions include the Cibolo Nature Center, Tapatio Springs Hill Country Resort, and Cascade Caverns.

Floresville, the Wilson County seat founded in 1867 by Canary Island immigrant Don Francisco Flores de Abrego, lies thirty-seven miles southeast of San Antonio. One of its early ranchers, Andrew G. Pickett, grew peanuts, widely cultivated in the county now. Cotton farming and cattle ranching diversified the area's economy in the 1900s. Floresville brands itself as the "Peanut Capital of Texas" and stages an annual Peanut Festival, a popular event that began in 1938. Floresville's population has increased from 5,868 in 2000 to 8,050 in 2023. The city's best-known native is John Connally, who served as governor of Texas from 1963 to 1969. Gov. Connally was riding with his wife, Nellie, in the convertible automobile with the president and First Lady Jackie when JFK was assassinated in Dallas in 1963. Connally, who also was shot, survived his wounds.

It's not just Austin and San Antonio that are booming. From Pflugerville to Floresville, the counties and towns surrounding the large core cities in the region are aggressively adding to their commercial and corporate portfolios. These cities have caught the eyes of commercial and residential real estate developers who are betting more people will be moving to the smaller cities surrounding Austin and San Antonio as the momentum of the two major metros is noted by residents and businesses from around the nation and the world.

The Emergence of a Central Texas Megaregion

We [mayors and county judges] want to make sure we have a broader view of what we are trying to accomplish. . . . We do not want to become "any town USA" and see all the boom and development without a sense of character and home. It has to be part of our calculus.

—Former San Antonio Mayor Ron Nirenberg

Core cities. Counties. Suburbs. They are all growing into a geographic cluster. But do they make sense as a cohesive economic region? Can so many distinct cities and communities spread over such a large geographical expanse find common ground? Austin, San Antonio, and the numerous other cities along the I-35 corridor and in the surrounding area are quickly filling out the regional landmass. This makes it increasingly easier to see it as a megaregion, a phrase that is working its way into the lexicon of civic and business leaders and residents.

The region is divided into two separate statistical metro areas, with San Antonio–New Braunfels forming the twenty-fourth-largest metropolitan statistical area (MSA) in the nation, while Austin–Round Rock forms the twenty-sixth largest. If Austin and San Antonio were defined as a single MSA, it would be the tenth largest. Dallas and Fort Worth were redefined by the US Census

Bureau as a single MSA in 1973. Today, Dallas–Fort Worth (DFW) is the nation's fourth largest. Neither Dallas nor Fort Worth lost their distinct identities in the process. Yet there is no denying their interdependence, also shared by the various surrounding cities and suburbs and knit together above all by DFW International Airport.

The US Office of Management and Budget (OMB), which defines metropolitan areas for statistical purposes, combined the Dallas and Fort Worth metros when it found the cities met the OMB requirement that 25 percent of workers living in one metro worked in the other. That pattern is evolving more slowly between the Austin and San Antonio metros. As noted in chapter 1, the two metros remain far from meeting the "employment interchange measure." Increasingly dense traffic is evident in all the cities and counties, worsened by the lack of mass transit options. Mobility is, perhaps, the most vexing issue that must be addressed.

It's reasonable to question whether Austin and San Antonio are a compatible fit culturally. The core cities are clearly different. Austin is younger and more hip. Austin looks toward California in attitude, educational attainment, and technology, even if conservative politicians in Texas often resort to shunning California as some sort of overpriced, unlivable, anti-Texas outpost. San Antonio looks more toward South Texas, the Gulf Coast, and Mexico, as well as to military traditions and its own rich Tex-Mex history.

People in the two cities don't necessarily see themselves living and working in an emerging megaregion. Austin is the state capital, which gives it statewide domain. San Antonio prizes its role as the dominant city of South Texas, presiding over a different region than Austin. With more than forty thousand residential properties titled to Mexican nationals, according to the Mexican Consulate in San Antonio, the city's reach into Mexico and its large population of bilingual, bicultural people is another important distinction with significant economic impact.

Fort Worth and Dallas were once distant neighbors too. Leaders in Fort Worth, a city that celebrates its cattle and ranch culture, at one time resented business-oriented, buttoned-down Dallas, but years of negotiation and compromise led to a working partnership. DFW International Airport was built in 1973. Today, it is one of the busiest airports in the world, with an annual passenger count exceeding seventy-three million, according to the Airports Council International. For decades now, the combined metro has served as a model of cooperation to the benefit of each city and all the metro cities surrounding them. The Mid-Cities, notably Arlington and Irving, have grown exponentially as well. Austin and San Antonio never found such common ground in envisioning the future of air travel.

Leaders in Austin and San Antonio are working to move beyond the distance that once separated the two cities in more ways than simply geography. Efforts at collaboration are being planted, but it remains to be seen if those seeds take root and bear fruit. Leaders in both major cities and the corridor cities realize the many opportunities that exist to play to one another's strengths, but the natural inclination is for leaders to put their cities first, the region second.

In the 1980s, for example, when Austin began to leap ahead in the computing technology industry, San Antonio also began its drive to excel and expand in biotechnology, and decades later, it created BioMedSA to measure and market its biomedical assets. It drew new investments. San Antonio leaders understood the value of cooperating with Austin's computing technology boom and had some success with companies like Rackspace, a San Antonio cloud computing giant.

San Antonio built and expanded its South Texas Medical Center, anchored by the UT Health San Antonio medical and dental schools.

Austin found itself as one of America's largest cities without a medical school. When Austin was selected as the home for the UT campus in the 1880s, state leaders decided to locate the university's medical branch in Galveston. In the early 2000s, Austin and university leaders collaborated to devise a plan to elevate Austin's place in the biomedical field. Residents voted in 2012 to raise property taxes to create a countywide health-care district, a medical school, a new teaching hospital, a community clinic network, and research and lab facilities. Collaboration in medical education now includes Austin Community College and Huston-Tillotson University. Construction and development continue at the UT Dell-Seton

Students walk along the Texas State University campus in San Marcos. Photo by Al Rendon.

Medical Center. Tech billionaire Michael Dell seeded the effort with a $50 million lead donation.

Some leaders in Austin tend to look down on San Antonio because of the Alamo City's lower per capita income and educational attainment and significantly higher poverty level. The Austin metro, after all, has more jobs with corporate pay levels and more jobs overall than the San Antonio metro, even though San Antonio's population is larger. Austin has more working people in the sixteen-to-sixty-four age range than San Antonio, which has larger portions of its population younger than sixteen and retirees older than sixty-four.

A difference in visuals may contribute to this. Austin's expanding skyline is impressive, at a distance and up close. San Antonio's downtown charms are found in its historic architecture and, below street level, all along the River Walk. San Antonio has the least impressive and most dated skyline of the top ten US cities. Locals and visitors alike are surprised when they reach the top of the

750-foot tall Tower of the Americas and gaze out at a seemingly endless horizon with no other buildings in the city reaching the same height. San Antonio in 2022 had thirty-one buildings taller than 200 feet. Austin had sixty-seven. Austin's newer downtown high-rise condominium and office towers loom high over the buildings that once dominated Austin—the state capitol building and the UT tower.

The difference in the cities' skylines may contribute to these impressions. San Antonio's lower skyline reflects the reality that it remains mainly a small-business city with few corporate headquarters, still catering to the visitor industry. H-E-B, the largest privately held employer in the state, with 145,000 workers, is based in a cluster of historic buildings located on the San Antonio River. It did select Austin as home to its new technology and innovation employment center, knowing that skilled software engineers were available for hire there.

Skyscrapers are built to suit large corporations and, when filled with marquee tenants, project business power and urban vitality. Perhaps San Antonio has been fortunate to have so few downtown

Caterpillar Inc. operates a heavy-equipment assembly plant in Seguin. Photo by Al Rendon.

towers now that cities across the country are struggling to keep them open with paying tenants in the postpandemic era. One of San Antonio's largest companies is the insurance giant United Services Automobile Association (USAA), which serves military families and their dependents around the world. At USAA's headquarters in northwest San Antonio, no part of the campus reaches higher than five or six stories. The Tower of the Americas was built originally as the defining landmark for HemisFair '68. Other highrise buildings hold historical significance and, by contemporary standards, are not really high-rises. The Milam Building, completed in 1928 at twenty-one stories and 208 feet high, was the first highrise in the nation to be air-conditioned, a technological advance that changed the future of economic growth in cities, especially in the South and Southwest. The distinctive thirty-one-story Tower Life Building, opened in 1929 at 404 feet, was San Antonio's tallest building west of the Mississippi and was the tallest structure in San Antonio until the Tower of the Americas was built. The Tower Life Building is being renovated by its new owner, Alamo Capital Partners, into a residential and mixed-use facility. Weston Urban is expected to do the same with the now vacant Milam. In 1988, two taller buildings than the Tower Life were added to the San Antonio skyline, the thirty-eight-floor Marriott Rivercenter Hotel at 441 feet and the thirty-two-floor Weston Centre at 444 feet. When San Antonio–based Frost Bank decided to replace its fifty-year-old office tower in the city, it commissioned Weston Urban and Pelli Clarke Architects to design and construct the skyline's first new tower since the 1980s at a relatively modest twenty-four stories. The bank's downtown Austin tower is thirty-three stories. The fact is, in contemporary times, San Antonio has never aspired to be the biggest city with the tallest skyscrapers in Texas. Instead, it values its status as the most inviting and historic city in Texas.

Linking the two cities, development will continue between US Highway 281 to the west and the SH 130 toll road to the east, with the I-35 corridor serving as the overtrafficked spine in the center. Land conservation efforts will be strong between US 281 and I-35 because of sensitive geological features, including the aquifer recharge zones and springs. If completed, the ambitious Great

Springs Project, a plan for undeveloped and lightly developed land west of I-35, will serve as a linear park between Austin and San Antonio offering residents a series of linked green spaces spanning one hundred miles for outdoor recreation and mobility void of motorized vehicle traffic. Open land between I-35 and SH 130 inevitably will see heavy commercial, residential, and industrial development.

Realistically, the two major cities and the growing corridor cities will continue to compete for economic development projects and urban amenities, though success in one city brings indirect benefits to the others. This competition-collaboration dynamic can be seen in two recent developments. One such example was the decision in 2019 by Major League Soccer (MLS) to pass over San Antonio and award an expansion franchise to Austin. With the Spurs owning San Antonio FC, a second-tier professional soccer team, it was assumed by many that the highly regarded ownership group supported by local elected leaders was in a strong position to win an expansion franchise. Austin, with no professional sports franchises, was seen as the Longhorns' turf, the sports monopoly belonging to UT. But Austin is the more affluent city with a stronger corporate base, and San Antonio's soccer stadium was located in the city's far northeastern corner. MLS prefers more urban locations. The subject is covered in greater detail in chapter 11.

A second example where rivalry trumped collaboration stems from the 2018 decision by the Pentagon to locate the Army Futures Command in Austin–San Antonio, although ultimately it didn't work out that way. In the initial bidding by thirty US cities, the Pentagon disclosed that San Antonio finished dead last on the list, principally because the University of Texas at San Antonio had not yet achieved Tier One status as a research university. Austin finished fifteenth. Its strength was UT, but it lacked the military medicine assets found in San Antonio. While the Army Futures Command's primary mission is advanced weapons development, a decision was made inside the Pentagon to place health-care and transition programs in the army under the new command.

Boston-Cambridge and the Research Triangle in North Carolina were seen as the two leading candidates for the new command, but the army allowed Austin and San Antonio to resubmit a single joint-city bid for a second round of bid reviews. The two cities, now united, finished first in the second round. Shortly after the announcement, however, Austin officials told Pentagon officials that UT's Dell Medical School could handle any liaison programming with the military. San Antonio was left on the outside. The command leadership eventually settled in offices on the University of Texas at Austin campus, but the advanced weapons testing site eventually went to College Station after Texas A&M University donated 103 acres of land and sweetened its offer by promising to construct a building designed for the army and its weapons testing. Austin won the command at San Antonio's expense, but ultimately, it saw little benefit. The Army Futures Command, never comfortable with its new mandate to expand into health-care management for departing servicemen and servicewomen, succeeded in getting military medicine transferred to the Pentagon's four-thousand-person Defense Health Agency (DHA), which began moving in 2023 from Washington to San Antonio, where many DHA civilian workers already are based. The city's ultimate success in winning this important mission and a new wave of federal civilian jobs occurred not because of collaboration but in spite of it.

If there is a lesson to take from the unraveling of the two cities' joint bid, it's that transparency and open communications will be essential to any future collaborations. Trust will have to be built over time and through the success of joint projects and initiatives. It will not be easy. When leaders in one city see the opportunity to seize an economic development advantage, it will be hard to resist.

Austin and San Antonio are growing into one megaregion by the measure of demographers, but the region's future depends on the hope that local elected officials and economic development agencies, when push comes to shove, will act in unity rather than in their individual city's best interests.

6

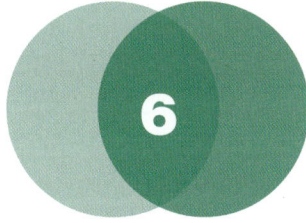

The Case for Multimodal Ground Transit and Enhanced Airport Collaboration

One of our greatest impediments to collaboration is not recognizing that our lives already are shared together, up and down I-35. We haven't talked about it. We haven't built a coherent strategy. It's happening around us. We have to maintain housing affordability. We have to address gentrification. We have to connect ourselves via transportation, and then I think our economic advantages are really going to shine here. We have such an incredible history. We have such incredible people.

—US Rep. Greg Casar (D-35), the only US representative from Texas whose district covers portions of both Austin and San Antonio

Transportation congestion is a problem created by success.
—Austin Mayor Kirk Watson

Transportation is the source of the greatest frustration of people living in this region.
—Former San Antonio Mayor Ron Nirenberg

I-35: There is simply no getting around it for the millions of people who live and work in Austin and San Antonio, not to mention the commercial traffic that plies the interstate from Laredo, the country's largest inland port and gateway to Mexico, now the

United States' largest trading partner. There are other byways, but to date, there is no practical alternative for the corridor cities and direct metro-to-metro traffic and commerce. And each of the byways has its drawbacks. The developing megaregion desperately needs a multimodal pathway to support a prosperous future. Today, the seventy-five-mile interstate that connects San Antonio to Austin via the increasingly densely developed corridor is a stop-and-go mix of commercial traffic traveling to and from the Texas-Mexico border, commuters who live in one of the megaregion's many cities and work in another, students attending one of the many colleges and universities that together enroll three hundred thousand within a one-hundred-mile radius, and the many people who travel within the region for business, shopping, or pleasure between the two big metros.

On a good day, fortunate commuters make the trek in about ninety minutes. On other days, highway expansion construction intended to improve connections to other expressways or one of the frequent vehicle collisions can force closures, with stalled traffic diverted to adjacent access roads. Anyone who travels regularly between the two cities has experienced delays that can turn the commute into a stop-and-go crawl. One example: On one August morning in 2023, a northbound pickup truck driver changing lanes in San Marcos and said to be recklessly speeding lost control and hit a tractor trailer and then another pickup truck. The first truck then flipped over the center median into the southbound lanes, striking a minivan. The second pickup was then hit a second time, this time by another northbound sedan. The pickup truck driver who caused the sequence of collisions and the minivan driver were killed, while numerous other individuals suffered non-life-threatening injuries. San Marcos police were forced to close both the northbound and southbound lanes for several hours. Frustrated drivers diverted to the access roads, took to their cell phones, and unleashed a torrent of angry social media posts. Yet the Texas Legislature months later began to allocate the state's record $33 billion surplus without any serious discussion or debate about funding transit alternatives in the corridor. It simply has not been a priority among the state's elected leaders.

Congested traffic moves slowly along I-35 in South Austin while never-ending construction to expand the interstate's capacity is underway. Photo by Benjamin Charles.

The congestion and the frequency of life-threatening collisions are only going to get worse as the population continues to grow and more and more single-occupant vehicles vie with big semitrailers for scarce space. Locally, elected leaders are now working to add double-decker lanes between or within the two metros, but few experts regard that as a solution. While the City of Austin will add double-decker lanes in the downtown area, the state has shown no inclination to adopt that strategy between the two metros. Transportation experts agree more lanes inevitably beget more traffic. Alternative transit modes are the only real option.

But more I-35 lanes remain the plan. TxDOT Executive Director Marc Williams said construction work snagging traffic on I-35 between Austin and San Antonio will never finish or end because of ever-rising traffic demand. "The work will never conclude on Interstate 35," Williams told a 2024 San Marcos transportation summit. Lanes can be added by elevated segments and lowered lanes within the existing right-of-way, Williams said.

The Alamo Area Metropolitan Planning Organization in San Antonio and the Capital Area Metropolitan Planning Organization in Austin both work with and depend on TxDOT, sales tax allotments, state and federal grants, and other revenue streams. Neither entity is a taxing authority; both lack the funding mechanisms to initiate transformational projects. Yet these organizations oversee I-35 in the megaregion.

"Transportation emerged as a critical issue after the passage of NAFTA [North American Free Trade Agreement, enacted in 1994]," observed Ross Milloy, Austin–San Antonio Corridor Council president. "We recognized right away there was going to be a challenge in addressing that. We are at the intersection of two interstates, I-10 goes east-west, while I-35 goes north-south. Eighty percent of Mexico's commercial output goes through Texas, 75 percent of that on I-35. All the studies we've seen show that no matter how many more lanes you add to I-35, it's always going to be congested. You have to start thinking about other alternatives."

For the many freight trucks that ply I-35 from Laredo to points north, there is only one other alternative highway, and few choose it. Based on TxDOT traffic counts, the vast majority of truckers continue to use I-35 rather than pay tolls on SH 130. The ninety-one-mile tollway is a sweeping bypass that connects at its southern point with I-10 near Seguin, looping north to Georgetown along Austin's less developed and populated eastern flank. As development accelerates to the east, SH 130 traffic will inevitably increase, but it remains to be seen if SH 130 will ever contribute significantly to a reduction in I-35 congestion.

Legislators in 2023 nixed a proposal to fund the construction of a connector highway linking I-35 and SH 130 between its north and south access points. "We are working on making a connector between I-35 in Comal County that would go over to SH 130," former New Braunfels Mayor Rusty Brockman said before the legislative session. Regional leaders believe the proposal will fare better in coming legislative sessions.

On the western edge of the megaregion, US 281 connecting to SH 290 offers an alternative to I-35 for some, particularly people arriving or departing from the relatively small, affluent communities

Passengers arrive at their destination by Austin's light-rail service. Photo by Al Rendon.

of Wimberley and Dripping Springs and other points along the western reaches of Austin. Increasingly dense traffic and highway construction through San Antonio's Stone Oak area north to Blanco, once a pleasant Hill Country drive, has become a more time-consuming backdoor route to Austin. It's not a practical option for time-constrained business commuters or commercial operators.

"Highway 281 is not a good route for freight movement. It has a lot of hills, and there is some very scenic countryside," Milloy said. "You have small towns that have their own character, their own sort of rural lifestyle. SH 130 on the eastern edge is designed to draw growth away from the aquifer, to draw growth away from the Hill Country. It is much more appropriate for a commercial route. Right now, SH 130 is tolled. I don't think it will be that way forever."

Amtrak offers twice-a-day service between the two cities, its trains running on the Union Pacific freight line, but the passenger carrier's on-time record is notoriously unreliable. Passenger trains are routinely redirected to side rails as freight traffic commands the right-of-way. Train travel postpandemic has become more expensive.

The bottom line: Austin–San Antonio is a megaregion that can't really function optimally as a unified region with a predictable flow of people, goods, and services without a major mass transit project supported by the state and the cities it would serve. The challenges are both financial and the identification of an efficient, available route. The topic currently isn't an agenda item for the Texas Legislature or TxDOT, which has not funded any intercity multimodal projects between Austin and San Antonio since the 2016 demise of the Lone Star Rail District. Realistically, even if the conversation begins in earnest now, it will likely take multiple legislative sessions to pass enabling legislation.

The failure to fund the Lone Star Rail project first proposed in 2003 represents a two-decade setback for rail advocates who see the need for congestion relief as an urgent priority. It's never been so for the state's elected leaders. The state's transportation agency has always kept its focus on building and expanding highways.

Transportation congestion "is a tough problem to solve because we love our cars," said San Antonio real estate developer and technology entrepreneur Graham Weston, "but it is a critical problem to solve. If we had a train or some way to zip back and forth between Austin and San Antonio, we would be a stronger, more competitive and prosperous region."

From the project's start in 2003 to its demise in 2016, serious planning was undertaken by the Lone Star Rail District to lobby city and state leaders for political support and funding. Over the years, $28 million was spent planning the passenger service. Knowing that mixing passenger and freight services on the same rail line often is dangerous, the rail district explored alternatives that included sharing Union Pacific's existing rail line's right-of-way or building a new, parallel rail line for Union Pacific. In the end, Union Pacific declined to share its right-of-way. It had too many commercial and industrial customers to service to risk delays by increased rail traffic. Funding was another challenge: The $2 billion estimated cost, a figure that now seems like a bargain, was deemed too expensive. The project was abandoned.

"The tracks controlled by Union Pacific and BNSF Railway, which have trackage rights in the Austin–San Antonio corridor rail, were built 150 years ago," Milloy said. He continued,

> The cities and towns grew up along those railroad tracks. At one time, that was the lifeline for those cities. What happens now, as freight carriers, [is that] they are very important to our economy. The truth is, freight carriers [are] going through the central parts of our cities. We don't think that's viable long-term. We think it makes more sense to convert those to passenger lines. The Biden administration recently passed several different measures that put a lot of money into rail infrastructure. Amtrak is receiving about $66 billion in the five-year plan. Of that, $26 billion [will go] into intercity rail. We would like to see Austin–San Antonio be part of that.

The quest has not ended for passenger rail service between Austin and San Antonio. In February 2024, Travis County Judge Andy Brown and Bexar County Judge Peter Sakai met with Union Pacific Railroad representatives in Washington, DC. The topic was a possible partnership to widen passenger travel through Central Texas, South Texas, and Mexico. Nothing concrete emerged from the meeting, but conversations continue.

> The real fact of the matter is, I don't think we have enough public resources to provide the infrastructure that we need. Now, I know this is going a bit against the stream of current thinking at the state level, but we've got to invite the private sector and to bring private capital to help build infrastructure that we need. We were in support of a bill during the 2023 legislative session that would allow the creation of a connector between SH 130 and Interstate 35 below New Braunfels. That bill was killed. We need to bring that bill back because we have to have that connectivity between 130 and 35. We have to enhance the other roadway.
>
> —Gary Farmer, Opportunity Austin chairman

Transportation "is a problem created by success. We're look-ing at more than $20 billion worth of infrastructure projects in Austin that are related to transportation," said Austin Mayor Kirk Watson. "It includes I-35, lowering it and adding some managed lanes, which will make a difference, not just for vehicular flow, but also for train and bus purposes."

Other ideas have surfaced. A first step to better public tran-sit in this region was proposed by the Alamo Area Council of Governments in 2022. The agency's pilot program aims to deter-mine whether buses could circulate twenty times a day between the two main cities with brief stops in New Braunfels and San Marcos. Fares could be $10 each way. Transit times, at least on good days, between the two main cities would be about ninety minutes. With broadband Wi-Fi service, passengers could use the time to work or relax. The pilot program would start with a modest $1.5 million budget in its first two years. If successful, the two transit agencies could apply for the rights to share a dedi-cated lane to shorten the transit time. This would make living in one city and working in another far more practical and better project a regional identity. Reliable, affordable passenger train service would unify the region and ease congestion throughout the megaregion.

"I think the challenge there is to have a single, continuous HOV [high-occupancy vehicle] lane between Austin and San Antonio on I-35," Milloy said.

"It is absolutely vital we continue the efforts to expand trans-portation service and capacity between Austin and San Antonio," Nirenberg added. "It will be part of the work that Kirk Watson and I and all the mayors along the I-35 corridor will undertake. The first step will be to ensure the VIA-Capital Metro vision is real-ized. Conversations about the expansion of transportation along the regional corridor must include how we connect our airports."

The building of a Toyota assembly plant in San Antonio in 2006 and a Tesla factory in southeast Travis County in 2020 has made the Austin–San Antonio region an automotive/transportation leader in a different way.

"The fact that we now are producing electric vehicles at Tesla puts us on the cusp of a transformation of the entire economy. It puts us on the cusp of every cutting-edge technology," Milloy said. "The strength is the people. Jobs don't go where there are no people, and people don't go where there are no jobs."

7

A Tale of Two Airports

Both Austin and San Antonio are interested in the expansion of air service capacity. The truth of the matter is that if we can fill in that middle, the ability to travel between Austin and San Antonio, you create a massive new potential for air service for people in the region. San Antonio has a strategic competitive advantage if you consider our San Antonio airport is in the heart of the city, but Austin-Bergstrom has done amazing work to expand service to Europe and other places. The opportunity to combine those strengths by making it easier to get from one airport to another is immense, and we shouldn't let that get by.

—Former San Antonio Mayor Ron Nirenberg

Airports and economic development are inseparable, especially in cities that attract millions of visitors or are home to global companies whose employees engage in extensive business travel. San Antonio fits into the first category, Austin the second. City and aviation leaders are challenged to anticipate business and consumer needs and demands in both growing metros. For cities like San Antonio and Austin that both compete for air travelers, they also must develop a culture of collaboration to maximize the potential for the two international airports that operate in the shadow of major hub airports, Dallas–Fort Worth (DFW) and Houston International.

Austin-Bergstrom International Airport (ABIA) opened in 1999, six years after the Base Realignment and Closure Commission ordered the closure of Bergstrom Air Force Base in 1993. At the same time it opened, Robert Mueller Municipal Airport was closed. Since then, ABIA has surpassed San Antonio International Airport in domestic and international routes. The growth of the city's tech economy and surge in business travelers has made ABIA more attractive to airlines. As a former Strategic Air Command base with the capacity to accommodate B-52 bombers, the largest aircraft in the air force fleet, Austin-Bergstrom has sufficient runway capacity to accommodate the largest commercial aircraft, which are capable of flying longer, intercontinental routes. ABIA now has nonstop flights to London, Amsterdam, and Frankfurt in Europe; Toronto, Vancouver, and Calgary in Canada; and Mexico City, Monterrey, Puerto Vallarta, Cancún, and Cozumel in Mexico. Other nonstop flights go to Montego Bay, Jamaica, in the Caribbean, and to Panama City and San José, Costa Rica, in Central America. Nonstop flights to Asian capitals are on the drawing board.

An American Airlines plane lands at Austin-Bergstrom International Airport. Photo by Benjamin Charles.

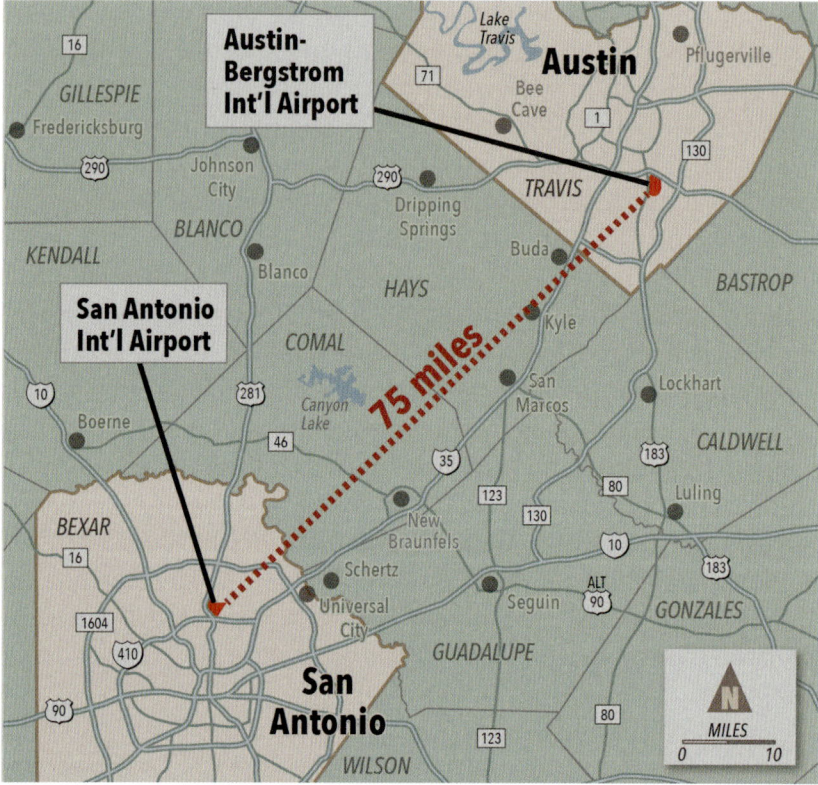

The two major area airports: Austin-Bergstrom International Airport operates on the southeast outskirts of Austin, while San Antonio International Airport is an inner-city airport. Austin's airport offers a larger number of domestic and international destinations for its large business travel market. San Antonio's airport offers domestic and Mexican international routes for its largely leisure travel market. The two airports could plan together to maximize airline service throughout the region. Map by Mike Fisher.

Despite its name, San Antonio International Airport is categorized by the National Plan of Integrated Airport Systems as a "medium hub" airport, with its limited nonstop destinations and many connecting flights routed through the Texas hubs as a "city airport."

Economic development leaders in the city have worked for years to secure nonstop flights to Europe or South America in addition to existing flights to multiple cities in Mexico. City and airport officials in 2023 announced that San Antonio would add nonstop service in the summer of 2024 to Frankfurt, Germany, on Condor, a lower-cost leisure airline with a Frankfurt hub that has received financial incentives from the city. The flights happened three times a week from May to September 2024. But passenger counts were low, and Condor canceled the second year of the planned two-year test period. San Antonio International's other foreign nonstop routes are limited to a handful of Mexican destinations: Mexico City, Monterrey, Guadalajara, Cancún, Querétaro, León, and Torreón. Some of those flights are seasonal.

In a long-sought, vital step for San Antonio and its airport, Congress in May 2024 passed legislation funding the Federal Aviation Administration that also opened the way for San Antonio nonstop flights to Ronald Reagan Washington National Airport. San Antonio had been excluded for decades by a Reagan Airport perimeter rule banning flights from more than 1,250 miles. Reagan is the nearest airport to Washington with quick and easy transfers into the capital. American Airlines was successful in winning the route. Previously, travelers to and from Washington used either Dulles International Airport or Baltimore/Washington International Thurgood Marshall Airport.

Austin and San Antonio serve different economies and different passenger constituencies, and therein lies the opportunity for future collaboration between the two airports. Competition for passengers and routes will continue. Both airports are in strong positions to grow as the megaregion grows, and as the fleet of commercial aircraft increases by 33 percent to thirty-six thousand aircraft by 2033, according to Airports Council International (ACI). The industry group also anticipates a nearly 6 percent increase in global passenger traffic between 2022 and 2040. By then, passenger travel is expected to grow to nineteen billion people passing through world airports.

San Antonio International has a new terminal on the drawing board, with completion set for 2028, yet concerns about the city's business composition and its per capita income levels could limit the airport's growth in nonstop international and domestic flights. The new San Antonio–Frankfurt nonstop service gives the city a chance to prove it has sufficient market demand for additional international flights.

For residents in the corridor cities, having two airports within commuting distance is advantageous. "I use both of them," said former New Braunfels Mayor Rusty Brockman. "We have international businesses located here. I am in a position to have the best of both worlds."

Talks between airport officials and business leaders can define what routes best serve the region and thus give both international airports more nonstop routes than they have now. As talks occur, they must look at various models of large metro areas that have multiple airports. Examples are abundant:

A traveler admires a large wheel of suitcases decorating a lobby at San Antonio International Airport. Photo by Audrey R. Rodriguez-Vallejo. Courtesy of San Antonio International Airport.

Dallas–Fort Worth: DFW International Airport and Dallas Love Field

Houston: George Bush Intercontinental Airport and William P. Hobby Airport

New York City: John F. Kennedy International Airport, LaGuardia Airport, and Newark Liberty International Airport

Los Angeles: Los Angeles International Airport, Hollywood Burbank Airport, Long Beach Airport, and John Wayne Airport

Chicago: O'Hare International Airport and Chicago Midway International Airport

Washington, DC: Ronald Reagan Washington National Airport, Dulles International Airport, and Baltimore/Washington International Thurgood Marshall Airport

San Francisco: San Francisco International Airport and Oakland International Airport

Miami: Miami International Airport and Fort Lauderdale–Hollywood International Airport

Each airport for each metro serves different roles in their regions. Other examples of multiple airports exist around the world. It is common for sprawling metros to have multiple airports, and it is common for coordination to exist between them in each metro. Coordination is what is missing in Austin–San Antonio now. Distance is one issue. Established traditions of economic competition are another.

The time has long passed on the proposal that Austin–San Antonio ought to build a single international airport located between the two metros. Corridor development has overtaken the ranchlands that existed into the 1990s. An Austin–San Antonio version of a DFW-like centralized airport, moreover, is not possible because DFW is only fifteen miles from the downtowns in each direction of Dallas and Fort Worth, while Austin and San Antonio are seventy-five miles apart, or at best about forty miles from each core city's downtown. Forty miles is too far for many residents or visitors to drive to and from an airport. Residents already are in the habit of deciding which airport is the most convenient for them.

An approach to determine the megaregion's air travel future could involve a formalized, regional airport coordination authority. The authority could be led by the Austin and San Antonio mayors, the Travis and Bexar County judges, the Austin and San Antonio city managers, and the two airport directors, among other possible local officials. This authority could follow, closely or partially, a federal model—namely, the Metropolitan Washington Airports Authority that oversees the Reagan National and Dulles International airports, which are 29.3 miles apart. The Washington, DC, area authority operates the airports, a toll road, and passenger rail service connecting the airports and also oversees their firefighting and police forces.

The authority is not taxpayer funded and is funded by airport landing fees, rents, and concession revenues. The authority uses bond issues based on its revenues to finance improvements and expansions. It has the power of eminent domain. The airport properties were transferred to the authority from the Federal Aviation Administration in 1987 through a law passed by Congress the year before. The authority has planned and constructed infrastructure improvements including new gates, checkpoints, runways, and an air traffic control tower. Dulles Airport's Aero-Train system began operations in 2010. Washington's Metrorail service was extended first to Reston, Virginia, in 2014 and then to Dulles Airport in 2022. The passenger rail route has eleven stations. Operation of the fourteen-mile Dulles Toll Road was conveyed to the authority in 2008.

The Austin and San Antonio airports will need the same kind of infrastructure planning for their future. Each city wouldn't have to give up control of its own airport, but a coordinating body could maximize the connectedness of the entire region. More could be built if resources are shared, although that may be more difficult because the Austin and San Antonio airports are farther apart than the ones closest to Washington, DC.

"We need to identify as organizations, as a collective megaregion, what are those top priorities. Then we need to advocate for that," said Jenna Saucedo-Herrera, greater:SATX president and CEO. "Historically, we have had priorities in San Antonio. Austin has had priorities. They have sometimes been aligned. Sometimes they haven't been. There is power and influence in the five million population that is expected to grow to more than eight million. We haven't been aligned around our priorities, around our plans. Now is the time to do that."

City and economic development leaders in both cities will undoubtedly be planning based on five airport megatrends outlined in a recent ACI report.

The five megatrends are as follows:

- Net-zero carbon emissions by 2050.

- Adoption of biometrics, artificial intelligence, automation, and machine learning technologies, especially for passenger processing.

- Improvements in intermodal connectivity linking city centers and airports and connecting airports, possibly through light-rail and even flying taxis.

- Efforts to overcome worker shortages to improve customer service and to provide training for new skills in engineering, digital, cybersecurity, and information technology.

- Advancing the "passenger experience revolution" through home and office luggage pickup, integrated travel apps, and wider passenger access to airline lounges, not just for the elite.

Airports will undergo fundamental redesigns in the coming decades. Like the megaregion itself, the airports we see today will bear little resemblance to the airports we will experience twenty-five years from now. But the two metros will each remain focused on their individual airports.

8

Securing the Water and Energy Future

What Austin and San Antonio have done, which makes this corridor a powerhouse, is the amount of land purchased to preserve water and water quality. I am proud of what this region has done in that regard. We're going to need to make sure we continue to do that.

—Austin Mayor Kirk Watson

I worry about the state. I don't worry about the city of San Antonio. That is because we have done a very good job over the course of the last three or four decades in not only managing and protecting the quality of the Edwards Aquifer and ensuring we are not pumping more than is sustainable but also in terms of investments in aquifer source recovery and desalinization as well as new regional sources.

—Former San Antonio Mayor Ron Nirenberg

We in San Antonio and Austin have to think about developing with nature, using nature and its features to filter water, mitigate the heat island, and help with air pollution. We have to build that into our network.

—Suzanne Scott, director of the Texas chapter of the Nature Conservancy

Austin relies on the Colorado River flowing through the Texas Hill Country into the Highland Lakes west of the city as its primary source of water. San Antonio historically has relied on the underground Edwards Aquifer as its primary source of water but has diversified significantly in recent decades and now only draws half of its water from the aquifer. Both cities share the rights to their respective sources of water, with other upstream and downstream cities and agricultural interests as well as other communities in the region dependent on the aquifer.

Securing the megaregion's future water supply first requires an understanding of the complex history of water rights that to this day are enshrined in Texas laws that treat surface water and underground water differently. Science and modern hydrology have long established the interdependence of underground and surface water. Water is water, regardless from whence it flows, but not according to Texas politics and law.

Early Spanish settlers in San Antonio built *acequias*, extensive systems of ditches to move surface water from its source—springs, rivers, and creeks—to where it was needed to irrigate crops and meet the needs of the pueblos and fields. These early water systems were managed locally by the people they served. Remnants of the acequias have been preserved and are still visible in various areas of San Antonio's historic neighborhoods, particularly in the World Heritage Mission District along or near the San Antonio River on the city's South Side. The Spanish tradition, known as prior appropriation, still prevails today. Put simply, it means "first come, first served." Today, "water rights" permits issued by the state assign water allotments to each stakeholder. Those who hold the oldest pumping rights, or senior rights, are first allocated their full allotment of water—even in times of drought—before junior rights holders draw water. If demand exceeds supply, as it increasingly does in cyclical droughts, it becomes a tale of haves and have-nots.

Arriving Anglos who followed the Spanish into Texas and eventually gained independence from Mexico had other ideas. They applied riparian law, which grants water rights to property owners along waterways. It is based on English law, and its primary flaw is that water is abundant in England and scarce in most of Texas.

Today, dual doctrine defines access to surface water in Texas, incorporating both historic approaches to water management. Basically, ownership of surface water in rivers and streams belongs to the state, while the rights to access that water belong only to those whose property holdings border the water and have permitted rights.

As more and more communities and landowners drilled wells, the state established the rule of capture, which means a property owner has the right to pump available water from underground aquifers. The water is treated like private property once it is pumped to the surface. Even the resale of such water is legal in Texas. There are limits now, as San Antonians learned when entrepreneur Ron Pucek opened the Living Waters Artesian Springs catfish farm southwest of the city in 1991 after drilling what the Edwards Aquifer Authority declared was the largest water well in the world. Pucek was pumping an astonishing forty-five million gallons per day, equivalent to what 250,000 people—one-fourth of San Antonio's population—were using at the time. A strong agricultural well might pump one hundred gallons a minute in much of rural Central or South Texas. Pucek's well produced forty-five thousand gallons a minute, yet his operation was legal.

As city and regional leaders came to grips with the situation and the public was drawn to daily news reports about the unprecedented pumping, the catfish farm served as a wake-up call that current regulations, or the lack thereof, could place at risk what at the time was San Antonio's sole water supply. Pucek was releasing the water into the Medina River after it flowed out of his catfish ponds, allowing authorities seeking a legal work-around to rule that catfish waste discharges were negatively impacting the quality of surface water in the river. That technicality allowed authorities to go to court and shut down Pucek's operation. The San Antonio Water System (SAWS) eventually acquired his property and water rights at a premium, paying him more than $30 million for water sales, leases, land, and equipment. It's of interest that individual right of capture is so deeply embedded in Texas law and culture that many other agricultural interests in the region thought Pucek was unfairly singled out and was well within his rights to pump as he pleased.

San Antonio has since taken steps to significantly diversify its sources of water, with the Edwards Aquifer now accounting for slightly more than half the city's supply. This chapter details those other sources. Austin still relies on the Colorado River and the Highland Lakes for its water supply but has set forth plans to diversify in the coming years, also covered later in this chapter. Moving from political intent to implementation will be a major challenge for the city, especially because diversification will probably not be accomplished before the next inevitable cycle of drought. The bottom line: Understanding the complex, some would say arcane laws governing water use must be considered in examining the necessary steps to secure the megaregion's water supply.

Far more area cities and communities than San Antonio rely on the Edwards Aquifer, so securing the region's water supply starts with protecting the environment by minimizing development over its sensitive recharge features—that is, how surface water flows into the aquifer and replenishes the water being pumped out. The aquifer is a vast honeycombed limestone formation recognized as one of the most productive artesian aquifers in the country. It's wrong, however, to think of the aquifer as "San Antonio's aquifer," even if no connection to Austin and farther north exists.

The Edwards Aquifer is constantly recharged by rainfall through a complex matrix of ground features such as creeks, sinkholes, caves, fractures, and faults. The Edwards extends under ten South Texas counties: Kinney, Uvalde, Zavala, Medina, Frio, Atascosa, Bexar, Comal, Guadalupe, and Hays Counties, an area approximately 180 miles long and 5–40 miles wide. The pioneer founders of Uvalde, San Antonio, New Braunfels, and San Marcos chose those locations because of the large springs that bubbled up and discharged from the aquifer. As the region grew, wells were drilled into the aquifer to supplement the springs, and today, the aquifer serves as the principal source of water for the region's agricultural and industrial activities while providing necessary spring flow for endangered species habitats and for recreational purposes and downstream uses in the Guadalupe, Nueces, and San Antonio river basins. Edwards water is so pure it does not require treatment other than the addition of chlorine for pipe sanitation and fluoride for community oral health.

From 2000 to 2020, the City of San Antonio used voter-approved sales tax revenues to purchase land or development rights over

Tubers and kayakers enjoy a float on the San Antonio River's Mission Reach. Photo by Al Rendon.

the aquifer's sensitive and fast-developing recharge zone. Over that time period, $325 million was used to protect almost 177,000 acres via 123 conservation easements and twenty-three properties purchased outright. The city now allocates $10 million from its annual budget to expand protected acreage from development. The previously used one-eighth-cent sales tax has been diverted to fund workforce-training initiatives for five years, and afterward, it will be reallocated to VIA Metropolitan Transit.

Austin does not pump water directly from the Edwards Aquifer. Yet the aquifer's sensitive recharge and contributing zones touch parts of Travis County. The San Antonio segment of the aquifer curves 160 miles underground from Brackettville in the southwest to near Kyle in the northeast, according to the Edwards Aquifer Authority. The Barton Springs segment extends from Kyle to South Austin. Recent research suggests the Barton Springs segment might be physically connected underground to the San Antonio segment.

People enjoy Austin's Barton Springs pool on a sunny summer day, sunning themselves on the slopes and taking a swim in the cold water. Photo by Benjamin Charles.

The Edwards Aquifer is divided into three main zones: the contributing zone, the recharge zone, and the artesian zone. The contributing zone covers 5,400 square miles of the Texas Hill Country, also called the Edwards Plateau, and extends east into Bexar, Comal, Hays, and Travis Counties. If officials look at the region purely from an underground water perspective, a megaregion already exists. The contributing zone is also called the catchment area. Annual rainfall averaging about thirty-two inches runs off into area streams and filters down through permeable cover. Development and impermeable cover impede the recharge, which is why limiting development over sensitive features is so critical to the future health of the aquifer. Water planning will become more important than ever as the region's population grows, development sprawls deeper into former ranchlands, and climate change renders the region hotter and more arid.

The largest water utilities in the region are Austin Water, a city-operated utility, and SAWS, a municipal utility that operates with its own independent board of trustees rather than as a city department. Austin's water sources are primarily man-made reservoirs, dammed lakes along the Colorado River. SAWS's sources are almost entirely underground aquifers. Austin Water operates three water treatment plants with forty-four pump stations to treat the surface water to drinking water quality. Historical threats to a clean water supply have included cyclical droughts, the need to protect endangered species in area springs, and population growth and development.

In the 1800s, the north-south dividing line known as the one hundredth parallel delineated between areas that received less than twenty inches of rainfall per year, to the west. That line was about ninety miles west of San Antonio. East of the line, rainfall was more than twenty inches per year. Landowners west of the line had more difficulty obtaining farm loans and crop insurance because of the lower rainfall levels.

Since the 1800s, however, the line gradually has been moved eastward, making more land in Texas arid. Experts now say the line has reached the ninety-eighth parallel, which is east of San Antonio and crosses directly through Austin. San Antonio's historical annual average rainfall is 32.38 inches. In 2022, the year's rainfall was only 11.51 inches. Austin's 2022 total rainfall measured 19.68 inches, the lowest total since 2011. A year does not make a trend, but it is increasingly clear that every drop of rainfall is precious, especially rainfall in thunder and lightning storms. Severe weather generates nitrogen that nourishes the roots of all vegetation. Sufficient rainy weather is necessary to preserve the area's tree canopy, which is essential to carbon capture and creating shade to mitigate the urban heat island effects that occur during the region's hot summers.

"We're going to see droughts worse than the drought of record [in Texas from 1947 to 1955]. That puts many, if not all, of our communities at risk of losing their entire water supplies during a new drought, even setting aside climate change. You look at tree ring data, how fat or thin the tree rings are. It tells you about past droughts," said Dr. Robert Mace, executive director and chief officer at Texas State University's Meadows Center for Water and the Environment. Mace added,

> There are megadroughts—that is, multidecade droughts—that affect this part of the state. Every community should plan for

the worst-case scenario. . . . I hope it doesn't come to that. You know that with the climate projections, different assumptions are made. I have faith in humanity that that will coalesce around this more than we have so far. I think, at this point, a best-case scenario for us is we probably will look more like Abilene, San Angelo. . . . It's very dry out there, which changes the makeup of the plant and foliage life, and other living things are impacted. . . . If developers don't have access to water, because communities are not going to allow builders to just tap into public water systems, they will have to bring some kind of water rights commensurate with what they want to build.

The Texas Nature Conservancy has acquired development rights to more than four hundred thousand acres of Texas land since 1964. "This can help families stay on their land. They can protect it. They can work it. People need nature, but nature needs people to make sure we can develop in the most sustainable way possible," Scott said.

"We need to find more water," Ross Milloy said. "The more near-term possibility is the conversion of brackish water. It's a much cheaper solution" than coastal desalination along the Gulf of Mexico.

Development is going to happen. You are starting to see this conflict where people are moving out to these places, the rivers, the open spaces, the dark skies. Development is starting to encroach on that way of life. Now people are seeing how to manage that growth. Let's develop as sustainably as possible. Let's build into the development practices that include more green space, more trees, and protection of the water. Make sure that instead of having boulevards and roads, you have buffer strips and places with water to be filtered before it gets into the aquifers. That means development may be more expensive in some cases, but it is like you are paying more now or paying more later.

—Suzanne Scott, Texas state director of the Nature Conservancy

We need "greater regional conservation as we work through the contours of Texas water law and as we put water where people aren't. That's the challenge. Because of the way our water law is structured, based on the rule of capture, it is not always true that populations are growing where the water supplies are. We have to figure out how to manage that and ensure that we have long-term water security in our population centers of San Antonio and Austin."

—Former San Antonio Mayor Ron Nirenberg

While San Antonio's population has doubled in four-plus decades, it today uses the same quantity of water as it did in 1980, thanks to conservation policies that included SAWS distributing more than one million free water-saving commodes to residents in the 1990s and, later, developing a number of alternative sources of water as well as underground water storage for later use in times of drought.

Until 1995, San Antonio relied exclusively on the Edwards Aquifer for its water supply. SAWS now sources water via fourteen projects from eight distinct entities.

San Antonio also has built a highly engineered network of pipelines that deliver recycled wastewater throughout the water utility's five-hundred-square-mile service area. The system enables the utility to eliminate the use of potable water for nonhuman consumption, such as CPS Energy, downstream industrial users, golf course irrigation, manufacturing operations, and other commercial and industrial uses. The system delivers what the state rates as Type I recycled water—physically, chemically, and biologically cleaned of all impediments and virtually indistinguishable from Edwards water. It's harmless to humans, yet it is not mixed into the water supply for human consumption.

San Antonio was the first major city in the state to approve and design a recycled water distribution system in 1993 when the SAWS board of trustees adopted its Water Conservation and Reuse Plan, which included recycled water as a component of the plan. Construction began in 1998, and the system became operational in 2009. It's often referred to as the "purple pipe system" for the distinctive color used by SAWS to distinguish the recycled water pipelines from others carrying water for household and office use. Threading a new pipeline system into the existing infrastructure of a modern city—already a complex layering of streets, water and wastewater pipelines, aboveground and underground electrical lines, flood-control tunnels, and more—was no easy task. Once built, the pipeline needed to connect directly to all its commercial users, from the Toyota vehicle manufacturing plant on the South Side to the TPC San Antonio golf courses at the JW Marriott San Antonio Hill Country Resort & Spa on the far North Side.

Currently, the recycled water is sourced from SAWS's Steven M. Clouse, Leon Creek, and Medio Creek Wastewater and Recycling Centers. In total, they generate 125,000 acre-feet annually. An acre-foot of water is equal to 326,000 gallons, enough to cover one acre of land one foot deep. Approximately 50,000 acre-feet of it is assigned by a contract to CPS Energy for use in its Braunig and Calaveras Lakes as cooling water at power generation plants. Approximately 50,000 acre-feet is assigned for downstream environmental streamflow. The remaining 25,000 acre-feet supply is for the recycled water program, which includes the San Antonio River running through downtown and the area's extensive creek system. Without that recycled water, the River Walk would be reduced to puddles in times of drought. The average San Antonio household uses 7,000 gallons of water annually, so the reclaimed water put back into reuse represents enough volume to service more than 114,000 households each year.

Austin Water's Reclaimed Water System is largely in the design phase, with a network of six major water mains serving different geographic sectors of the city. The system is expected to be completed in 2026.

SAWS is recognized as the state's leader for its water diversification projects that have reduced the city's sole-source reliance on the Edwards Aquifer. The first diversification project occurred in 2002 with an agreement to pump water from the Trinity Aquifer to serve northern Bexar County. That supply accounts for less than 2 percent of San Antonio's water supply, but it was the first non–Edwards Aquifer water, and it set a precedent for diversifying the water supply, which met initial resistance from ratepayers and other regional communities. The opposition came from fears that turning to surface water supplies would relax aquifer protections and conservation efforts.

Starting in 2008, water purchased from Schertz and Seguin has been pumped from the vast Carrizo Aquifer to SAWS's H2Oaks property in south Bexar County. A desalination plant completed in 2016 elevates the brackish water to drinking water quality, accounting for 5 percent of the city's water supply. Its location also saves SAWS from maintaining hundreds of miles of new pipeline to serve the region's growing population. Injection wells that SAWS has developed on the site now are used to store unused water pumped from the Edwards Aquifer in "wet years," as well as excess water from its newest project, the $2.8 billion Vista Ridge Pipeline. Currently, SAWS's wells hold enough water to supply the city for one year.

The Vista Ridge Pipeline project was developed between 2014 and 2020 in partnership with private developers who built a 142-mile pipeline from Burleson County northeast of Austin after obtaining pumping rights from dozens of private agricultural wells that draw from the Carrizo-Wilcox and Simsboro aquifers. Vista Ridge now accounts for up to 30 percent of the city's water supply. Coincidentally, the Vista Ridge Pipeline runs parallel to I-35 for a significant part of its length.

SAWS officials expect the Vista Ridge Project to deliver more supplemental water than San Antonio needs now or in the coming years, and it remains possible other corridor cities will seek to purchase the excess supply to diversify their own water sources and protect their communities in future drought cycles. Pumping privately sourced water from aquifers located 147 miles northeast of San Antonio, however, makes it more expensive than existing water sources. To date, there have been no secondary buyers. SAWS officials believe continued population growth and the inevitable cycles of severe drought will create demand and help underwrite the cost of the $2.3 billion project.

For all its conservation efforts, the city and SAWS still allow commercial and residential property owners to plant non-native turf and install automatic irrigation systems prohibited in some Southwestern cities. That points to an obvious, if politically unpopular, opportunity for local officials to mandate greater conservation efforts by prohibiting non-native grass species and implementing further restrictions on landscape irrigation. "About 50 percent or more of the water used in the hot summer months goes to landscape and lawn irrigation," said SAWS Chief Engineer Greg Eckhardt.

"The least expensive water is the water we never use, the water we conserve," said SAWS President and CEO Robert Puente.

Austin's fast-growing population coupled with the prolonged 2008–16 drought in Central Texas reduced the Highland Lakes to near-historic lows and convinced officials they risk running out of water in the future unless new sources are found and additional conservation efforts are implemented. That led to the development of Austin's Water Forward Integrated Water Resource Plan, which aims to meet the city's water needs. The plan calls for new conservation measures, still undefined, and citywide installation of smart meters and improved water-saving irrigation systems. It proposes a city ordinance requiring new homes to have native grasses and plantings and more drought-tolerant landscapes. Commercial and industrial operators will be required to connect to the city's reclaimed water distribution system once it is completed. Austin also intends to follow San Antonio by establishing injection wells for storing water collected in wet years to be used in times of drought. The city's updated one-hundred-year plan calls for the construction of a brackish water desalination plant to process water to be acquired from the Carrizo-Wilcox Aquifer. This would represent the first supply of drinking water to Austin pumped from an underground source.

The Texas Water Development Board is keeping an eye on how the state can apportion and share water supplies over the coming decades and studying future projects that could follow the Vista Ridge Project, the first project of its kind in Texas that transports water from a less populated rural area with less pressure on its underground water supply to a major urban population in a more drought-prone region. More water, for example, from East Texas could eventually move in pipelines to the west.

Both cities have set ambitious goals to achieve carbon neutrality in the coming decades. The Austin Climate Equity Plan, adopted by the city council in 2021, calls for carbon neutrality to be reached by 2040. San Antonio's SA Climate Ready Plan sets a 2050 deadline. Environmental groups say neither city is likely to achieve its goals by those dates. Austin Energy and CPS Energy in San Antonio share a valuable commonality: Both are municipally owned utilities rather than investor-owned utilities. Ratepayers are the shareholders. Reliability and affordability, rather than profit, are the key drivers for energy executives. That has led to lower utility bills than those experienced in Texas cities with investor-owned utilities. Citizens also enjoy a far greater voice in influencing elected officials and utility trustees to diversify energy portfolios and set target dates to shut down coal-fired plants in favor of renewable energy sources, including solar and wind.

It's interesting to compare the energy source portfolios for both utilities (see table 8.1).

Undeveloped lands to the east of the two cities present prime locations for the construction of new solar-generation fields. State leaders and municipal utility operators, still at odds over the billions of dollars in debt incurred by energy utilities during Winter Storm Uri in February 2021, saw how solar-generated energy prevented the potential collapse of the state's energy grid during the 2023 record heat waves and energy demand for air-conditioning. Cities

Table 8.1.

Power source portfolio for two utilities

Source	Austin Energy	San Antonio CPS Energy
Renewable energy (wind, solar, biomass)	50%	10%
South Texas Project nuclear plant near Bay City	22%	25%
Coal	17%	25%
Natural gas	11%	31%
Purchased power from other sources	9%	

Sources: Annual reports and websites.

in the corridor could collaborate on the establishment of such fields, perhaps in concert with landowners and private-sector solar farms, and deploy the energy regionally as needed.

The two energy utilities have a history of working together. Along with Houston, the two cities participated in the 1970s construction of the South Texas Project (STP) nuclear plant. Austin Energy owns 16 percent of STP, which accounts for 22 percent of its power generation. CPS Energy owns 40 percent of STP and derives 25 percent of its power from nuclear. Without Austin Energy choosing to participate, CPS Energy pursued the expansion of the nuclear facility for nearly a decade in the early 2000s, but in 2017, utility leaders finally wrote down nearly $400 million invested in the project. Government and public support disappeared in the years following the Fukushima Daiichi nuclear disaster in Japan in 2011. A tsunami caused by the worst earthquake in the island's history destroyed the plant and took almost twenty thousand lives and required the evacuation of nearly five hundred thousand people. Almost all the victims actually died from drowning, but the catastrophic nature of the event sent shock waves around the world, especially in Europe, where Germany later declared its intent to wean its country from all nuclear-generated power, even as France and Spain continued with plans to build more nuclear power plants. Only one recorded death was linked directly to radiation release at the plant, but the impact on the nuclear sector and public opinion was generational. CPS Energy subsequently turned to an energy conservation program and larger investments in natural gas and renewable energy sources, wind and solar, to expand its capacity and accommodate growth in its service area that extends well beyond the city of San Antonio. Smaller, less expensive nuclear plants are now under development and could lead to an eventual renewal of public support for nuclear power, which is unlikely to occur anytime soon, if at all.

Today, both utilities have diversified energy portfolios that increasingly depend on solar and wind to supplement fossil fuel–generated energy. Austin is ahead of San Antonio in its use of wind and solar, but San Antonio generates a higher percentage of its energy portfolio from nuclear, so both cities have different energy generation profiles as they work to implement their respective plans. The transition to carbon neutrality will not be easy, and there are many doubters. As climate change contributes to more extreme weather events in Texas in both summer and winter, many believe peak power demand on the state's energy grid will preclude dismantling gas-powered plants.

City officials are under constant pressure from renewable energy advocates to accelerate plans to abandon coal-generated electricity. CPS Energy plans on converting its Spruce II coal plant to gas in 2027 and "mothballing" its Spruce I coal plant in 2028. Austin Energy missed its self-imposed 2022 deadline to withdraw from joint ownership of the Fayette Power Project coal plant near La Grange by year-end 2022 after it was unable to reach an agreement with its partner and fellow plant owner, the Lower Colorado River Authority (LCRA). The Fayette Power Project continues to operate because of the Energy Reliability Council of Texas's urgent need for electrical generation, with a new goal of Austin Energy leaving the project by 2029. LCRA plans to continue operating the Fayette Power Project after Austin Energy leaves the coal plant partnership.

Being municipally owned instead of private-investor owned exempts the two power utilities from certain requirements for competition in Texas' deregulation law passed in the early 2000s. Areas in the Austin–San Antonio metros not covered in Austin Energy's and CPS Energy's service areas are served by small municipal utility districts that mainly use natural gas turbines to generate electricity.

Renewable energy storage for distribution when the wind is not blowing or the sun is not shining is a focus of development efforts to match generation capacity with demand at both Austin's and San Antonio's utilities. Plans for solar panels and wind turbines include efforts to make them environmentally friendly.

"It gets back to planning," said Scott. It's "how to think development can happen with nature and not against nature. You [can] incentivize development to go in places where it would move away from these sensitive areas. You have to make sure that renewable energy is placed where they don't take away from the migratory paths or the beautiful viewsheds in river systems."

While both energy utilities work to implement their plans, transportation-generated greenhouse gasses represent the biggest single obstacle to achieving carbon neutrality. Texas and California alone account for 20 percent of the country's transit-related emissions, according to the US Department of Transportation. In Austin, 46 percent of emissions come from buildings, while 26 percent come from transportation, which includes personal and commercial vehicles, public bus transit, and trains. In San Antonio, the numbers are 44 percent for buildings and 40 percent for transportation.

As the region's population growth continues at a record rate, water and power conservation are imperative in the Austin–San Antonio region, where cyclical droughts and extreme summer and winter temperatures will further test the state's much-criticized energy grid. Millions of Texans lost power and water in Winter Storm Uri. The counties that bothered to report storm-related fatalities put the death count at 246 people who succumbed to the freezing temperatures and lack of heat, a number public health officials consider an undercount. Ratepayers were left owing billions of dollars for natural gas purchases acquired by desperate utilities at record prices during the massive blackout. Subsequent lawsuits have charged private natural gas sellers with price-fixing and preying on vulnerable populations. Lawmakers have taken modest steps to weatherize more energy-generating plants and to incentivize more gas plant construction, but Texas remains highly exposed to weather events and climate change that will continue to challenge the reliability of power and the availability of an adequate water supply.

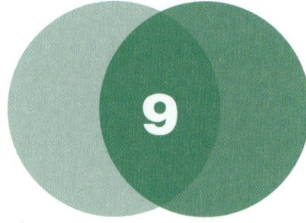

A Cruel Mismatch

Housing Unaffordability and Wage Inequities

The pandemic did not slow down the extraordinary growth in population and economic development in our region, and we did not slow down in our mission to expand the base of affordable housing in our community and to provide critical services to move low-income people to greater self-sufficiency.
—Michael Gerber, CEO, Housing Authority
of the City of Austin

The affordable housing waitlist numbers have increased by nearly 200 percent since the onset of COVID-19 in San Antonio. Nearly 100,000 of our San Antonio families, which equals to almost 250,000 people, are on an Opportunity waitlist. If these numbers aren't startling, I'm not sure what is.
—Michael Reyes, public affairs officer, Opportunity Home
San Antonio, and the OHSA appointee to
the Mayor's Housing Policy Task Force

Austin and San Antonio and the corridor cities face a housing crisis on multiple fronts. Both major cities—in partnership with housing authorities, developers, and nonprofit organizations—are taking unprecedented steps to address the crisis. Each major metro has launched a ten-year plan to address the growing gap in the supply of market-rate and affordable housing and to address homelessness. Yet the affordability gap continues to grow. Housing starts simply cannot keep pace with the influx of new residents to the region. Competition for scarce housing, inflation, and high interest rates have combined to make owning a home impossible for more and more families. Renters face the same scarcity as fewer new multifamily developments are coming online. The bottom line: More and more families in the megaregion are spending more than 30 percent of their household income on housing, a redline for housing experts who say that places household stability at risk. Families who spend too much of their take-home pay on housing have insufficient resources to meet other necessities: food, clothing, health care and childcare, transportation, and utilities.

"Texas urban cities pride themselves on the economic boom," said Nicole Nabulsi Nosek, chair of the nonprofit Texans for Reasonable Solutions. "The boom will come to a bust if employers and employees run out of homes to live in, akin to California's mistakes in chasing out their middle-class families and their workforce in droves by making it harder to build Missing Middle housing."

"The numbers are startling," wrote Ed Hinojosa Jr., the president and CEO of Opportunity Home San Antonio (OHSA), formerly known as the San Antonio Housing Authority, in an August 2023 op-ed published in the *San Antonio Express-News*. "We need bold, decisive and ambitious action to make real, sustainable inroads in providing quality housing that our fellow residents can access and afford."

Hinojosa noted that the housing authority has received no funding from the city or county since its inception in 1937. Local housing authorities do not receive state funding either. Most funding comes from the US Department of Housing and Urban Development. Other municipalities outside Texas do fund local housing authorities, augmenting the federal funding.

"Cities such as Boston and Portland already invest in their future by allocating an annual appropriation to their housing authorities to maintain and modernize existing affordable-housing stock," Hinojosa wrote in the op-ed. "Policymakers understand that quality housing is the foundation for economic mobility and growth. It is the foundation for families to achieve better health, education, and financial outcomes."

By 2024, the City of San Antonio began allocating $1 million in annual funding to the housing authority.

Rapid population growth continues to outpace housing starts. That demand-supply imbalance drives up prices. Texas had around twenty million people in 2000. It surpassed thirty million in 2022 and is on track to grow to fifty-five million by 2050. Building permits for both single-family and multifamily housing continue to lag behind population growth.

The number of people living below the poverty line in both cities contributes significantly to the housing crisis. Among the nation's ten most populous cities in 2022, San Antonio had the third-highest poverty rate, with 17.7 percent, according to the US Census. Only Houston and Philadelphia had higher percentages. The official poverty measure is $13,465 for a household of one. Austin's poverty rate is only 12.4 percent, below the state average of 14 percent. While Austin has fewer people living in poverty, the more rapid increase in housing costs for both homeownership and rentals has driven more and more people into financial crisis.

"If Austin and San Antonio are to build an economic corridor, it will need affordable transit and housing," Reyes said. "San Antonio, arguably, continues to have affordable housing options, while Austin is struggling to keep up the pace with its growth, which has stifled its housing options. Herein lies an opportunity. Conversely, San Antonio continues to struggle in building a solid corporate base, whereas Austin is successfully doing so. This, too, offers an opportunity. The missing pieces are transit and housing. I think most policy observers understand this, but the problem is so much larger than these two missing components."

The numbers for the lowest income groups are less dire in Austin, no comfort to families who find themselves unable to find affordable housing. The Austin City Council implemented new regulations to change minimum single-family home lot sizes from 5,750 square feet to 2,500 square feet in 2023, allowing for greater residential density with the construction of more affordable multifamily units, townhouses, and backyard casitas. Another initiative would allow developers to build up along major thoroughfares where developers have been constrained by height limitations.

According to the resolution approved by the Austin City Council, home prices rose by 55 percent from 2010 to 2020, with a 20 percent population increase during that time period. Homeownership for middle-income earners plunged from 50 to 28 percent over the same decade.

City councils in both major cities have eased zoning restrictions, allowing so-called accessory dwelling units, commonly called "casitas," located in backyards or atop the garages of single-family residences, to increase density and the number of affordable market-rate housing units. As Austin was passing its resolution in July 2023, San Antonio announced a citywide design contest for the most innovative designs in casita construction and cost.

The two issues of greatest importance for most in the housing and rental markets are affordability and availability. The COVID-19 pandemic propped up vulnerable renters and others with the flow of federal stimulus funds that also brought a temporary halt in utility service disconnections and evictions. Widespread job loss in the service industry put many hourly wage earners at risk of losing existing housing once eviction restraints on landlords were lifted and utility cutoffs resumed. The issue is likely to be subject to court challenges for some time, but state legislators have moved to block cities from enacting new postpandemic bans on evictions as part of a broader effort over the last decade to limit home rule cities from enacting ordinances that are contrary to legislative initiatives to limit municipal authority.

First-time homebuyers, meanwhile, face affordability challenges. In a study conducted by Clear Capital, a real estate data provider, Austin was ranked as the number-one city for rising median house prices from 2005 to 2020, with values rising 6 percent annually, while San Antonio ranked number five at 4.5 percent. Over the same period, median household income in Austin rose by 3.2 percent annually versus 2.4 percent in San Antonio, according to the latest five-year US Census Bureau American Community Survey. Housing prices spiked further during the pandemic. Inflation, meanwhile, is driving up labor and material costs and slowing new housing starts, hurting first-time homebuyers seeking to buy in a now less affordable, entry-level subdivision. The Federal Reserve's efforts to contain inflation with a two-year sequence of interest rate increases have made interim financing for developers more costly and placed the cost of mortgages beyond the grasp of many, even households with two professional wage earners. The median price for a single-family house in Austin was $530,000 in 2023, which actually represents a 5 percent drop from 2022. The median home price in San Antonio was $315,000, about 3 percent less than in 2022. In both instances, however, the median prices represent steep rises in value and cost over the last decade.

The growing number of families who can no longer afford to buy a home has led to higher rental costs as more individuals and families compete for scarce units. Many multifamily developments in Austin's and San Antonio's urban cores are now priced at levels many residents cannot afford, pushing them farther out in search of more affordable housing and thus raising the time and cost of commuting to and from their jobs. In other instances, it has resulted in overcrowding as multiple generations have no option but to live in the same home. The median cost of a one-bedroom rental unit in Austin in 2022 was $1,595 per month, which would require an individual to earn $63,800 in order not to exceed the standard 30 percent income-to-rent affordability ratio. Austin's 2022 per capita income was $41,761. In San Antonio, a resident needs to earn $44,167 to afford the median price for a one-bedroom unit of $1,049 a month, but the per capita income was only $31,148 in 2022.

Rising rent costs have caused more and more low-wage workers to struggle to stay housed, and as a result, waiting lists for public and subsidized housing have increased. Both Austin and San Antonio report growing homeless populations, and a rising number of families have faced eviction or otherwise are at risk of losing their housing due to financial problems. Both cities are struggling with an increase in homeless tent encampments in urban areas, which lead to higher crime rates and prompt forced sweeps by local authorities.

The Housing Authority of the City of Austin and OHSA both face far greater demand than they can meet now or in the near term. In fact, both housing authorities face a growing population of families requiring public housing or housing vouchers that are simply unavailable. Both cities are seeking to devise new funding mechanisms to accelerate the construction of affordable housing and the acquisition of existing properties for conversion to subsidized housing. City and housing leaders are acquiring former hotels and multifamily properties to serve the unhoused with affordable housing or transitional housing. Still, both cities struggle with more people on the streets, more homeless encampments, and the deadly impact of fentanyl among drug users living on the street, many of whom suffer serious mental health conditions and resist entering city shelters or cannot meet sobriety and medication protocols to access services. Both cities struggle to provide sufficient detoxification beds in shelters. Both cities have insufficient transitional housing for individuals and families ready to exit shelters.

In 2023, the US Department of Housing and Urban Development (HUD) included Austin and San Antonio on a list of twenty-nine cities that received multimillion-dollar grants aimed at reducing the growing unhoused populations. Austin received more than $7 million, while San Antonio received $14.5 million. The awards were in addition to the multimillion HUD grants the cities receive annually to provide housing and other services for the homeless.

Housing density could rise in Austin's future because of the $7.1 billion Project Connect approved by voters in 2020 to expand mass transit projects. Austin is hoping for assistance from the Federal Transit Administration (FTA) to cover about half of the Project Connect costs and discovered that its score for its FTA application would rise if the city had denser housing patterns. In December 2023 and May 2024, the Austin City Council approved the two phases for an effort called HOME Initiative, intended to create denser housing. The first phase allows for up to three housing units on many lots. The second phase shrinks from 5,750 square feet to 1,800 square feet as the minimum size of a lot for one housing unit, according to the *Austin American-Statesman*.

Hourly wage workers earning less than the median household income are especially vulnerable in an economy that sees people at the top and in the upper-middle class thriving, while hourly wage workers see stagnating pay and rising housing, food, and health-care costs undermining their stability. A growing number of middle-class and college-educated salary workers—teachers, police, firefighters, and others—say they can no longer afford to live in the cities where they are employed, which results in longer, more costly daily commutes.

Rental affordability is a nationwide problem, but Texas ranks as the sixth-worst state for available affordable housing, according to the National Low Income Housing Coalition (NLIHC), which identifies Austin and Dallas–Fort Worth tied as the third-worst metros in the country and Houston as the fourth worst. San Antonio is more affordable and not ranked among the nation's top ten worst metros. In all, there are only twenty-nine available residential units for every one hundred renters in Texas, according to NLIHC's 2023 report. In Austin and San Antonio, the availability is twenty-one per one hundred and thirty-one per hundred, respectively. That adds up to a shortage of 77,618 additional rental homes in the San Antonio–New Braunfels metropolitan statistical area (MSA) versus 256,485 in the Austin–Round Rock MSA, according to the coalition.

All these numbers indicate the problem is especially acute in Austin, even as the city experiences yet another tech boom, highlighted by thousands of workers being hired to work at Tesla's GigaTexas factory and its battery production plant outside the city. High-wage earners are supplanting low- and middle-income families in inner-city neighborhoods, causing those housing prices to skyrocket. By one market estimate, 25 percent of all homes for sale in Austin in July 2023 were priced at $1 million or more.

"The ongoing displacement of our working-class population is a very serious concern," Austin City Council member José "Chito" Vela told Bloomberg News. "We need to build housing."

Austin ranks at or near the top of the list of thriving US cities, but Austin's untold story is one of inequality and the continuing displacement of the city's isolated working-class Latino community, which was traditionally concentrated in modest housing east of the I-35 interstate. As gentrification overtook those East Side neighborhoods, steep increases in housing values and ad valorem taxes forced out working-class families and led to a redevelopment boom with many new upscale multifamily units, mixed-use developments, and trendy bars, restaurants, coffee shops, and boutiques moving in among the housing stock and Latino-owned retail businesses. In truth, census data using the Gini coefficient, a commonly used measure of statistical dispersion that reflects the degree of inequality in a metro area's income distribution, show Austin and San Antonio are nearly identical. The takeaway here is that as the state's demographics reflect a fast-growing Latino population and a decreasing Anglo population, income inequality will only become more pronounced, presenting city and housing officials with an intractable challenge.

Austin's housing crisis was an issue for both candidates in the 2022 mayoral election between state Rep. Celia Israel and former state Sen. Kirk Watson, who prevailed narrowly in the December vote. Both candidates were pushed hard to propose specific housing plans. With 114,167 votes cast, Watson, who previously served as the city's mayor from 1997 to 2001, eked out a win by an 886-vote margin.

"This is going to be the new status quo," Ben Martin, a senior research analyst for the nonprofit advocacy group Texas Housers, told the *Texas Tribune*. "The challenges and suffering that were occurring for people with the lowest incomes is just now continuing to climb up the income ladder and being felt more directly by a broader swath of residents."

Outdated building codes in both cities have contributed to the housing problem. Changes in zoning restrictions are being vigorously debated—and often resisted—that would allow more affordable housing developments in many affluent neighborhoods. The City of Austin introduced CodeNEXT in 2012, which ultimately fell short in updating the land development code that regulates land-use and building parameters. The city's Imagine Austin plan adopted that same year called for "sustainability, social equity, and economic opportunity; where diversity and creativity are celebrated; where community needs and values are recognized; where leadership comes from its citizens, and where the necessities of life are affordable and accessible to all."

The Austin City Council adopted a Strategic Housing Blueprint in 2017, which lays out a ten-year plan to create sixty thousand affordable housing units. By 2022, the Austin City Council was implementing significant land-use and building code changes. Yet developers in Austin and San Antonio are struggling to provide affordable housing units in their projects that qualify for various tax credits and subsidies. It's difficult, developers say, to find enough public incentives to break even financially, much less make a profit.

San Antonio remains an affordable alternative to Austin, yet lower wages mean many people are being priced out as more and more people are unable to afford the rising cost of market-rate apartments. Leilah Powell, executive director of Local Initiatives Support Corporation, identifies a gap of 150,000 units in San Antonio.

In 2018, former Mayor Nirenberg led the effort to create and fund a major affordable housing initiative in the city. The effort gained momentum in 2020 when voters approved a charter amendment allowing housing to be included in the city's five-year bond cycles for the first time. Yet the housing crisis deepened with the COVID-19 pandemic, with tens of thousands of people thrown out of work and thousands of families saved from eviction and utility disconnections, thanks to moratoriums and federal rent subsidies funneled to cities. Four years after the Austin City Council approved its ten-year Strategic Housing Blueprint in 2017, the San Antonio City Council followed suit in December 2021 with the establishment of a ten-year Strategic Housing Implementation Plan (SHIP). Voters in 2022 then overwhelmingly approved the allocation of $150 million in bond funding for the city's comprehensive housing initiative (see table 9.1). The city is allocating the funds to private and nonprofit entities whose proposed projects have been approved by a citizens committee in a competitive review process.

The SHIP has five overriding goals: (1) coordinate housing initiatives among local government entities, nonprofits, and private-sector developers; (2) increase city investment in housing; (3) increase affordable housing production, rehabilitation, and preservation; (4) protect and promote neighborhoods; and (5) ensure accountability to the public. The city's Affordable Housing Dashboard allows citizens and the media to track progress,

Table 9.1.

Allocations from the $150 million San Antonio ballot initiative

Ballot initiative	Allocation
Buy and build rental housing	$35 million
Help homeowners undertake critical and energy-saving repairs	$45 million
Acquisition and rehabilitation of affordable housing	$40 million
Supportive housing services	$25 million
Home construction	$5 million

Source: City of San Antonio Strategic Housing Implementation Plan.

and its Housing Base website helps renters find affordable rental units in the city. Housing officials say $150 million is only a start, and much more private-sector investment will need to be leveraged. Voters will be asked in 2027, the city's next bonding cycle, to continue funding the SHIP.

Austin's Affordability Unlocked Plan was launched in 2019 to ease zoning restrictions in urban core neighborhoods and to incentivize developers to pursue greater density in projects that include affordable units. San Antonio's Infill Development Plan was passed by the San Antonio City Council in 2018 to create infill development zone and mixed-use zone changes allowing for greater density in inner-city neighborhoods. Both plans share the same goals: greater neighborhood residential density, relaxation of parking restrictions, the move to smaller single-family home lots, and increased heights. Whether the private sector can provide the housing remains an open question.

The limited public funds available to address the housing crisis mean there will be no quick fixes. NIMBYism, the tendency of established residents to adopt "not in my backyard" opposition to affordable housing projects, too often blocks efforts to achieve greater residential density in the form of almost any variation of multifamily housing. As a result, achieving affordability to address homelessness, displacement, and gentrification becomes difficult.

Small houses built by Lennar in Converse are part of the San Antonio area's efforts to provide affordable housing. Photo by Al Rendon.

Small residences are sold in Austin's Community First! Village to address the megaregion's need for affordable housing. The village is in East Austin. Photo by Benjamin Charles.

As of this writing, the housing crisis in the two metro areas was growing worse, despite these efforts. Much more will need to be done as populations swell and the competition for both market-rate and affordable housing grows.

Like virtually every other US city, Austin and San Antonio face serious challenges managing homeless populations. Each city conducts an annual point-in-time study that seeks to measure both subsets of the homeless population: those living in shelters and availing themselves of wraparound services and those living outside shelters who are more resistant to intervention. In January 2023, Austin/Travis County reported 2,374 unhoused individuals, including 1,108 people using temporary shelters and 1,266 unsheltered and living in encampments in parks, under overpasses, and in greenbelts. The San Antonio count found 3,155 people in Bexar County were experiencing homelessness, including 874 people unsheltered and 2,281 sheltered. Officials in both cities said the number of homeless families with at least one child had shot up 60 percent since the pandemic's moratorium on evictions ended, and steep hikes in the cost of rent caused more people to lose housing. While the total number represents a 5 percent increase in the homeless population since the 2022 count, 16 percent fewer individuals were living on the streets. Officials in both cities say the point-in-time counts are accurate snapshots but ultimately produce an undercount of how many people over the course of the year experience homelessness. The officials also estimate that at least 4,000 or more people are unhoused over the course of a year.

Both cities have funded postpandemic programs to expand available beds in emergency housing shelters where nonprofit agencies operate "low-barrier" admission facilities for chronically homeless individuals, often in former motels. The centers allow individuals who will not enter sobriety programs. San Antonio's nationally recognized Haven for Hope campus downtown at one point in 2022 counted more than 1,600 residents, some sleeping on office floors because of a shortage of beds and dorms. More than 180 nonprofit partners offer an array of therapeutic, medical, dental, and other essential services at Haven for Hope, but residents must become sober to qualify for residency. The city-owned Austin Resource Center for the Homeless serves 130 men who are not required to be sober, while the county-owned Austin Shelter for Women and Children, operated by the Salvation Army, has eighty-one beds also serving low-barrier residents.

In Austin, one innovative response to the homeless crisis has been the creation by the nonprofit Mobile Loaves and Fishes of a fifty-one-acre, five-hundred-home campus that now houses more than 350 people in permanent housing structures that include 110 mobile homes, 200 microhomes, and shared facilities such as laundry, outdoor kitchens, community food gardens, and coworking spaces. Tenants pay a small amount of rent based on their income and also perform work on the campus to maintain the facilities.

In San Antonio, the former Towne Twin Drive-In movie theater has been turned into Towne Twin Homes on the city's East Side, which opened in 2023 and is supported by the Housing First Community Coalition and other local nonprofits. Its mission is to provide permanent housing for two hundred people who are homeless and disabled in RVs, mobile homes, and small houses. Residents will pay 30 percent of their income to live there. SAMMinistries, a nonprofit that provides housing and services to people experiencing homelessness, purchased the sixty-unit Hudson Apartments on the city's near–North Side in 2021 and is now remodeling eighteen of the units to be ADA compliant. Both projects offer residents wraparound services such as supplemental food packages and sobriety meetings.

Homeless officials in both cities cite the need for more transient housing and more psychiatric and detox beds for individuals seeking help. The issues of homelessness and the mental health crisis visible in so many US cities are not unrelated. Bexar County Sheriff Javier Salazar has told county commissioners that about 230 jail inmates face indefinite incarceration because they have been deemed unfit for trial, while a dearth of available beds in psychiatric hospitals prevents their transfer from incarceration to care.

It isn't just a big-city problem. San Marcos Police Chief Stan Standridge, Hays County District Attorney Kelly Higgins, and other local officials formed the Hays County Behavioral Advisory Team in March 2023 with the intent of reforming the county's behavioral health services. The Hays County Commissioners Court has reacted favorably to the plan put forth to build a diversion center for individuals with mental health issues. The plan also calls for the creation of a city-county Behavioral Health Office to divert emergency mental health calls away from San Marcos police and county deputies to mental health experts. At this stage, the plan is not funded, but the very fact that it is a stated priority sets an example for other corridor cities that face the same challenges.

Austin and San Antonio might look to Houston for other ideas and approaches. Houston officials are credited with moving more than twenty-five thousand homeless people back into apartments and houses rather than shelters or other transient facilities. The Houston mayor and Harris County officials, working closely with the nonprofit Coalition for the Homeless, have been cited by federal housing officials as the place with the most success in reducing its homeless population and best succeeding in putting individuals back into permanent housing and keeping them there. Houston does not practice zoning, which makes building certain types of housing easier anywhere in the city. Houston city government prioritized for housing programs federal funding received for Hurricane Harvey relief and COVID-19 relief. The city also created a command center for the allocation of funding for social services aimed at the homeless.

While some cities continue to debate the efficacy of "housing first" approaches to homelessness, Houston was able to streamline the process for all the various entities addressing some aspect of homelessness to work more closely in unison. The results have been dramatic. But the approach requires far more available housing and funding than either Austin or San Antonio has identified to date. The two cities will find that working on expanding the inventory of affordable housing and addressing growing populations of unhoused adults and children will remain major challenges as the regional population continues to grow at record rates. Officials in both cities and in the corridor cities who have not worked together closely on homelessness and housing in the past will have to do so to better address housing needs.

Housing affordability can be a negative factor for a city's economic growth because young professionals cannot move to a city that is too expensive. Working families sometimes are forced to look for less expensive housing in other regions. Housing is at the center of a region's critical concerns. In the worst case, expensive housing could be a limiting factor in a region's continuing growth.

10

Austin and San Antonio Transformed Economic Development Strategies and Then Grew Closer

We are very different in many ways, but we have some similarities that we can work on, use that diversity to our advantage.
—Gary Farmer, Opportunity Austin CEO

It's a matter of coming to the table and having our respective organizations like Opportunity Austin and greater:SATX operationally aligned and working together. They're having conversations, but convening to develop a plan with deliverables and timelines and accountability is how we continue to push our megaregion forward.
—Jenna Saucedo-Herrera, president and CEO, greater:SATX

Austin and San Antonio have been two of the fastest-growing cities in the country over the last decade, and demographers see the region continuing to lead in population and job growth. That growth has accelerated in the new century for good reasons. For some years now, Austin has been cited in various surveys as the number-one desired destination for job-seeking college graduates. That is not simply because of the city's profile as an inviting university town with a great music and festival scene, although that is what attracts many people in the first place. San Antonio, where the largest employer for most of the second half of the twentieth century was Kelly Air Force Base (Kelly AFB), underwent profound social, racial, and economic changes in the late 1960s and 1970s and staged HemisFair '68 to celebrate the city's 250th anniversary and its historic role as a crossroads. The fair was creatively themed as the "Confluence of Civilizations."

US Rep. Henry Gonzales, the first Latino elected to the Texas Senate and US Congress, was the first to suggest a world's fair as a coming-out party for the fast-growing city. Its success marks the beginning of San Antonio's modern era and its continuing efforts to shake off its legacy as one of the nation's poorest cities to one with a more diversified, equitable economy; greatly improved racial and ethnic relations; and better education outcomes. Yet poverty persists.

Today, Austin and San Antonio consistently finish in the top five largest US cities for job and population growth, a barometer that has to be seen as an affirmation of both cities' economic development strategies.

Austin

Growth over the last two and a half decades in Austin was spurred by intention. Civic and business leaders came together in 2002 to pull the city out of the dot-com bubble burst, or at the time what they called Austin's "tech wreck."

"Up until the tech wreck, Austin's economic development was very laissez-faire," said Gary Farmer, the founder of Opportunity Austin, which launched under the umbrella of the Greater Austin Development Corp. in 2003. "The city didn't have a plan. The Austin Chamber of Commerce didn't have a plan. No one had a plan."

The new entity was created to raise the city's profile nationally as a city with a highly educated labor force in a business-friendly state with no income tax and an affordable cost of living compared to tech-centric cities on the East and West Coasts. Farmer is widely credited as the visionary and driver of Opportunity Austin and is now widely consulted by economic development leaders in other cities.

Market Street Services, a community and economic development consultancy that has worked in 160 cities in thirty-four states, was hired to conduct a market study of Austin's strengths and weaknesses and to examine how business leaders outside Texas viewed the city. What Austin leaders learned from the study, Farmer recalled, was that no one knew much about the capital of Texas, and what they thought they knew was wrong.

"Until then, through the eighties and nineties, there were lots of up and down cycles but no outreach strategy. If a company wanted to come and set up here, fine, but we didn't go looking for companies," Farmer recalled. "And nobody mentioned Austin in the same breath as Silicon Valley or Boston. We knew we were a tech town, had been since the eighties, but nobody else knew. Most Fortune 500 company leaders outside Texas who were surveyed thought Austin was an oil-and-gas town. So job number one was to establish our identity. We launched our first five-year plan in 2004. Today, we are in the final year of our fourth five-year plan."

Opportunity Austin's new plan called for devoting half of the revenue it raised from private-sector members to the recruitment of out-of-market companies and working to retain companies in its five-county metro area. Thirty percent was dedicated to improving education outcomes in Austin's primary and secondary public schools, with a goal of sending more high school graduates to college and encouraging more college students to pursue advanced degrees in science, technology, engineering, and mathematics. Funding also was allocated to more direct workforce-training programs to increase the number of skilled workers with dual credit/certification credentials. The funds to support Opportunity Austin were raised from private-sector chamber members.

Additional funding was spent on advocacy for infrastructure improvements, notably roadways, and improvements at Austin-Bergstrom International Airport (ABIA), which opened in 1999. That included "hard costs" in the form of payments to airlines to establish international flights to destinations other than Mexico. At the time, there were about thirty nonstop domestic flights out of ABIA. Today, there are about one hundred nonstop destinations, including fifteen international flights to London, Frankfurt, Amsterdam, Panama, and Mexico City. More are on the drawing board, with airport traffic growing as Austin attracts more and more high-paying jobs and young professionals with disposable income. Austin-Bergstrom attracts double the annual passenger count of San Antonio International Airport.

Market Street's work included a competitive analysis with cities like Phoenix, Nashville, and Portland and helped Austin realize the potency of its location, with more than three hundred thousand students enrolled in colleges and universities within a one-hundred-mile radius of the city.

"One thing and one thing alone carried Austin forward: talent and its educated workforce," Farmer said. "And God blessed us with a very nice canvas on which to paint. Austin is a very nice place to live."

Farmer noted the impact of former state Sen. Kirk Watson (D-Austin), who first served as Austin mayor from 1997 to 2001 and would later be returned to that office by voters in 2022. Watson worked successfully as a state senator to secure highway funds to start to address Austin's worsening traffic issues in those early years.

"I'm a Republican and a supporter of Gov. Abbott," Farmer said, "but the governor will tell you he regards Kirk, a Democrat, as one of the most effective people to have served in the Senate." Watson served in the Texas Senate from 2007 to 2020.

Opportunity Austin's track record induces envy in other cities. Over nineteen years, from 2004 to 2023, the five-county metro attracted 827 new companies and created 40,400 new jobs, said Farmer, making the Austin area the number-one job creator on a percentage basis in the United States over that period. The newest major tech company to plant its flag in Austin is Tesla. Tesla founder Elon Musk first announced plans in 2020 to build an electric truck manufacturing plant in Austin. The following year, he decided to move Tesla's corporate headquarters from Palo Alto, California, to Austin. What had begun one year earlier as a $1.45 billion investment and promise of 500 new jobs quickly grew in scale. By 2023, with the expansion of the Tesla pickup truck factory and the establishment of a nearby vehicle battery factory, the company's local investment had grown to $5 billion and 12,000 jobs.

"*Jobs for families, returns for taxpayers, opportunities for companies*—those nine words are the best description of Opportunity Austin," Farmer said with pride.

The gigantic Tesla GigaTexas factory operates on the southeastern outskirts of Austin. Photo by Larry D. Moore (Wikimedia Commons, CC BY 4.0).

Watching Austin's phenomenal job growth in recent decades belies the fact that it all began with a single typewriter manufacturing factory established there by International Business Machines (IBM) in 1966. From its original workforce of three hundred producing Selectric typewriters, IBM has since evolved from typewriters to mainframes to desktops to systems management and consulting, a global tech giant and one of Austin's top ten employers, with a workforce of six thousand. IBM proved to be the first of many companies that established operations in Austin and helped create its high-tech manufacturing sector.

One year later, Infotronics and Communications Research arrived, then in 1968, Texas Instruments. Westinghouse came in 1971. In 1972, the Austin Chamber worked with officials in nearby Seguin to recruit a Motorola auto parts manufacturing facility. Two years later, Motorola selected Austin for a semiconductor plant. Eagle Signal, which manufactures computerized traffic control systems, came in 1975. Data General and Advanced Micro Devices arrived in 1978. In the space of less than twenty years, 11 percent of the Austin workforce was employed in tech and advanced manufacturing. Today, that figure has doubled to 22 percent.

San Antonio

Economic development in San Antonio in the second half of the twentieth century was born out of necessity. City leaders could see the phenomenal growth underway in Dallas and Houston, while San Antonio remained one of the country's poorest cities, with an economy dependent on its military installations and the post-HemisFair tourism boom. Yet for all its River Walk allure and charm, San Antonio also was defined by decades of local government disinvestment in the city's West Side, South Side, and East Side, where the largest concentration of people of color lived. Such institutionalized inequities made San Antonio one of the most economically segregated cities in the country. Everything in the city, it seemed, was separate and unequal, with a traditional old-style leadership structure somehow enjoying near-total economic and political control. Before San Antonio could develop economically, it needed to develop in other ways.

Change was led by San Antonio native and economist Ernie Cortez, founder and head of Communities Organized for Public Service (COPS), a grassroots organization of twenty-six parishes in the low-income Latino inner city, which began operating and organizing in 1974 the first Industrial Areas Foundation organization in Texas. Cortez and COPS devised creative and persistent ways to pressure Anglo civic and business leaders to end the practice of ignoring communities of color when it came to public expenditures and capital improvement projects like flood-control and street improvements. Public school funding was distributed unequally too, which only deepened segregation and unequal education opportunities and outcomes, with Bexar County serving as home to twenty school districts. COPS wanted a seat at the negotiating table when the time came to allocate scarce resources, and it won that seat and used it to great effect. COPS's peaceful, proactive protests led to profound changes in the city and the adoption of a new ethos of racial and ethnic collaboration and political representation. Under pressure from the US Department of Justice, San Antonio adopted single-member districts in 1977, bringing to a close the end of the Good Government League, a closely knit group of business leaders who handpicked candidates for city council. City council representatives started to better reflect the city's racial and ethnic makeup as Blacks and Latinos won seats.

Newcomers to San Antonio were not burdened with the historical biases of local city fathers and served as catalysts for change. Air Force Brig. Gen. Robert P. McDermott—a Boston native, a World War II fighter pilot, and the first dean of the US Air Force Academy—came to San Antonio in 1968 to serve as chairman and CEO of the United Services Automobile Association (USAA), the insurance company formed to serve active duty and retired military officers. "McD," as he was universally known, assumed a leading role as a civic transformer and in 1974 led the effort to create the San Antonio Economic Development Foundation (SAEDF). It would serve the city well in the post–Cold War era when all four branches of the US armed forces underwent significant downsizing and mission change.

By the advent of the 1990s, San Antonio's leaders knew economic diversification loomed as a more urgent challenge. One was the fear that San Antonio's diverse military installation posts could be targeted by the Pentagon's Base Realignment and Closure Commission (BRAC), which began its work to downsize and consolidate military installations after the end of the Cold War. Tourism and conventions provided a steady stream of visitors and income, but the related service jobs were low paying. The city's bilingual population attracted multiple back-office service centers, but again, the wages were low, and the jobs were mostly filled by people whose schooling ended at high school. The University of Texas at San Antonio, the city's first four-year public university, was only founded in 1969, and its first graduating class in 1973 included only eighty-two students. The lack of a Tier One public university would hold the city back for decades.

The BRAC announced its first round of base closures in 1988 and proceeded to announce subsequent rounds in 1991, 1993, 1995, and 2005. These five BRAC rounds led to the closure of 350 military installations and an annual savings of $12 billion annually. San Antonio's number came up in 1995 with the announcement that the air force would close Kelly AFB, one of the nation's four major

military logistic hubs. Mayor William Thornton raced to Washington and successfully lobbied Clinton administration officials to go
slow, buying the city more than five years from the announcement
to its actual closure. Still, the challenge was unlike anything the city
had faced in contemporary times. And by the time Kelly was winding
down its missions, the commission announced the planned closure
of Brooks Air Force Base in 2001, home to aerospace medicine in
San Antonio. The closure of Kelly and Brooks served as a tough,
one-two punch to the city's economy and its identity as Military
City USA. San Antonio is still home to Lackland and Randolph
Air Forces Bases (AFBs) and the army's Fort Sam Houston and
Brooke Army Medical Center, best known for its world-class burn
treatment and research hospital. City leaders suddenly were con-
fronted with the need to replace more than twenty-five thousand
civilian jobs that had paid federal wages and over the previous half
century proved central to the establishment of the city's Latino
middle class.

Mario Hernandez, the longtime president and CEO of the SAEDF,
saw the city through these difficult years, including the Great
Recession in 2008. He served for a record thirty-two years at the
helm of SAEDF, during which time San Antonio saw the arrival of
a Toyota truck assembly plant on the city's underutilized South
Side, the significant growth of insurance and banking giant USAA,
the establishment by Microsoft of a data center, the growth in the
number of cybersecurity firms, and the opening of major corporate back-office service centers.

The decision by Toyota to encourage the formation of multiple
Latino-owned suppliers whose operations would be located at the
South Side plant was a boost for both the Japanese automaker
seeking to enter the Latino truck-buying market and a network of
Latino business leaders who invested in the supplier chain.

The 1992 initialing of the North American Free Trade Agreement by President George H. W. Bush, Mexican President Carlos
Salinas de Gortari, and Canadian Prime Minister Brian Mulroney
took place at the city's historic German-English School. Cross-
border trade between Texas and Mexico grew exponentially from
the mid-nineties into the next decade. San Antonio's location along

A Toyota Sequoia SUV rolls off the assembly line at San Antonio's Toyota assembly plant. Photo courtesy of Toyota Motor Manufacturing, Texas.

I-35 proved advantageous as Laredo, the gateway city to the south along the border, boomed as the nation's most active inland port.

The National Security Agency (NSA), with less public fanfare, established a new base in a former Sony chip manufacturing plant. Today, NSA San Antonio is the largest signals intelligence facility in the United States outside of NSA headquarters in Fort Meade, Maryland. The NSA facility, combined with intelligence gathering operations underway at Lackland AFB, gave birth to what today is the city's growing cybersecurity industry, now centered at Port San Antonio on the former Kelly AFB and the adjacent Lackland AFB.

San Antonio's biosciences sector continued to attract talent and government contracts. The Texas Biomedical Research Institute was engaged in world-class research of infectious diseases and viruses. The nonprofit BioMedSA was founded in 2005 to accelerate the growth of the health-care and biosciences sector, create regional economic benefit, and contribute to the health of San Antonio and beyond by establishing San Antonio as a leader in health care and bioscience. The nonprofit VelocityTX was established on the city's near–East Side in 2017 as a subsidiary of the

Texas Research & Technology Foundation. Its Innovation Center was established to help companies launch, win funding, and connect to other collaborators through the nonprofit's database of three hundred companies in the biosciences space.

VelocityTX had already outgrown its space in the former Merchant Ice House building, now outfitted with state-of-the-art clean rooms for biosciences research. An adjacent building is under development. By 2023, 160,000—one in six adult workers—employed in the city worked in the medical, health-care, and biosciences sector.

San Antonio's economy was no longer largely solely dependent on the military presence and the convention-and-visitor industry. Still, local business leaders couldn't help but watch with envy as Austin secured one significant economic development win after another. They began to discuss a more ambitious strategic plan.

USAA executive Wayne Peacock served as chairman of SAEDF and led the national search for new leadership to follow the retired Hernandez. He found a next-generation leader right in San Antonio. Jenna Saucedo-Herrera, a member of the SAEDF board and a CPS Energy executive who had yet to turn thirty, was named the new president and CEO of SAEDF in 2016. She wasted no time in implementing a change agenda, first by moving SAEDF's offices out of the downtown Paseo del Rio, where the Greater San Antonio Chamber of Commerce was housed. At the time, SAEDF was seen by some industrial prospects outside the city as an extension of the chamber and municipal government. In a city with more than a dozen chambers of commerce representing diverse racial and ethnic groups and geographic entities, Saucedo-Herrera sought to redefine SAEDF as an independent organization with a distinct regional outlook and deep private-sector engagement. She introduced the idea of a new name and branding campaign; too many assumed that SAEDF as a "foundation" must have had significant financial resources to disburse when, in fact, its annual $2.5 million operating budget trailed badly behind counterparts in the other large cities.

Saucedo-Herrera established new offices on a high floor of the Weston Centre with a panoramic downtown view, a far more impressive venue for welcoming visiting brokers and company representatives exploring a possible move to San Antonio. The building is owned by billionaire Graham Weston, a cofounder of Rackspace and the leading force in downtown development through Weston Urban, his real estate company.

Saucedo-Herrera's "coming out" as the SAEDF CEO was staged at the Pearl Brewery, a former vacant industrial wasteland transformed into one of the most admired adaptive reuse projects in the country, with a Culinary Institute of America campus, numerous high-end restaurants, upscale apartments and offices, the Pearl Stable event center, a weekly farmers' market, and a regular schedule of pop-up arts and social events. The constantly evolving campus included the 2015 opening of the celebrated Hotel Emma in the long-vacant landmark brewery building. The Pearl was the vision of billionaire Kit Goldsbury, whose fortune was built on the successful sale of Pace Picante Sauce. He ignored the advice of many real estate and development experts when his investment arm, Silver Ventures, acquired the Pearl, at the time an abandoned eyesore. Its success would transform the entire River North area between downtown and the upper reaches of Broadway, coinciding with the redevelopment of what is now known as the Museum Reach of the San Antonio River. A stretch of San Antonio that was once home to blight, vagrants, and street prostitution is now a showcase destination and home to thousands of young professionals and affluent empty nesters. The Pearl attracts high-end travelers who come to San Antonio for the city's distinct culture, Mexican influence and *ambiente familiar*, and vastly improved and diversified culinary scene. San Antonio has moved well beyond traditional Tex-Mex *comida* and is now recognized as a UNESCO City of Gastronomy.

In ramping up greater:SATX's ambitions, Saucedo-Herrera won the backing and financial support of the city's most important next-generation business leader, Peter J. Holt, the third member of the Holt family to serve as chairman of Spurs Sports & Entertainment, who also serves as CEO and general manager of HOLT CAT, the country's largest Caterpillar dealer. With funding from USAA and Holt, others soon followed, and the greater:SATX budget grew to $9 million by 2023.

Saucedo-Herrera knew that the office move, while an important symbolic message, was only a first step. She needed a strategic plan, a well-articulated business plan, and a supporting cast of private-sector leaders—city builders and job creators—to do more than attend board meetings. Over time, she assembled a who's who of business, academic, and local government leaders, and together, they engaged the same company as Austin, Market Street, to formulate a new strategic plan that included a name change. SAEDF would now be known as greater:SATX.

Craig Boyan, president of H-E-B, whose headquarters is located on the former historic US Army Arsenal campus on the San Antonio River, was an early recruit to the leadership team and served as board chair. H-E-B's expansion into North Texas and its continuing growth on both sides of the border and into northern Mexico had made it the largest private grocer in the United States and the largest private employer in Texas, with more than 145,000 "partners," as it calls its employees and executives.

Another key supporter was Weston Urban CEO Randy Smith, whose firm completed the Frost Tower in 2019, the first new high-rise on the city's downtown skyline since 1989. The tower was the centerpiece of a public-private partnership that Weston Urban successfully proposed to the City of San Antonio and Frost Bank in 2014. It involved a sequence of center-city property and building transfers and a commitment to add hundreds of new residential housing units downtown, all in return for significant incentives. The city acquired the former twenty-two-story Frost Tower, and after its renovation as the newly named City Tower, the city was able to consolidate employees previously dispersed at five different sites. Through the public-private partnership and other acquisitions, Weston Urban launched new construction plans and redevelopment projects over a twenty-three-acre expanse of the western reaches of downtown, including the thirty-two-story 300 Main residential tower opening in 2024. As more tech start-ups and workers flocked downtown, Weston and other former Rackers, many now leading successful start-ups, launched the nonprofit Tech Bloc to give tech-sector workers their own organization and to create an effective lobbying entity at city hall.

Bexar County, meanwhile, undertook the $300 million restoration of historic San Pedro Creek, which runs for 2.2 miles through the western downtown and south to its confluence with the San Antonio River.

Another board member and key driver behind the development of the new strategic plans was Michael Lynd Jr., founder and CEO of Kairo Residential, which is best known for its significant multifamily development holdings in Chicago, Miami, Denver, and Austin. His company is partnering on the construction of a seventy-four-story mixed-use tower in downtown Austin. Lynd also serves as the chairman of the Alamo Regional Mobility Authority and is a prominent voice in calling for new financial mechanisms to address the region's growing transportation challenges.

Bryant Ambelang, CEO of Silver Ventures, and Brandon Gayle, COO of Spurs Sports & Entertainment, are also executive committee members. Holt and the Spurs recently diversified their investment group, which now includes tech billionaire Michael Dell in Austin, where the Spurs are popular and now play several regular-season games annually.

Many of the San Antonio business leaders working with greater:SATX also formed a large ownership group to acquire the San Antonio Missions, a Double-A minor-league franchise. Civic and business leaders are exploring the possibility of a new downtown sports and entertainment district that would become home to the Spurs and the Missions.

Two key wins for greater:SATX were the decision in 2017 by New York–based EY (formerly known as Ernst & Young) to establish its second-largest national office in San Antonio, with 1,200 employees providing cybersecurity and financial services, and the move by the global wealth management firm Victory Capital, one of the Fortune 100's fastest-growing companies, to relocate its corporate headquarters from Cleveland to San Antonio in 2019.

As 2020 approached, with the pandemic not yet on anyone's radar, San Antonio civic and business leaders focused on new approaches to build on the success of landing Toyota fourteen years earlier and expanding advanced manufacturing, the growing number of cybersecurity firms, and the opportunity to attract more aerospace jobs and defense work to Port San Antonio. The city needed a smart jobs growth strategy and needed to make sure it was doing everything necessary to support and retain local employers.

The Market Street survey of San Antonio confirmed for Saucedo-Herrera and others at greater:SATX what they already knew: San Antonio was best known as the home of the Alamo, River Walk, and other tourist attractions like SeaWorld and Fiesta Texas. A great place to visit, but was it a great place for business investment? Did it have a skilled workforce? The name change from SAEDF to greater:SATX helped launch a new regional development strategy in 2022, delayed by the pandemic, yet rolled out with substantial support from the city government, the many local chambers of commerce, and major employers.

A variety of company relocations handled by greater:SATX include several that expanded upon the region's burgeoning vehicle manufacturing base of Toyota and Caterpillar. AISIN Texas Corp., a maker of vehicular automatic transmissions and a subsidiary of AISIN AW Co., set up operations in Cibolo with 900 planned jobs. Navistar International Corp., the former International Harvester, created 700 jobs with a plant turning out commercial trucks and buses on San Antonio's South Side and expects its workforce to grow to 1,000. The British forklift company JCB in 2023 announced a new factory in San Antonio that would create 1,500 jobs in five years.

San Antonio's civic and business leaders are working to expand San Antonio International Airport, which has experienced growth in passenger traffic and an expansion of routes. Yet the city-managed airport struggles to attract and retain nonstop routes so preferred by travelers; airlines often cut back service when the economy slows. Many San Antonians found it faster and more economical to travel to Austin for flights out of Austin-Bergstrom. San Antonio's population was significantly larger than Austin's, but the number of business travelers and individuals with sufficient disposable income to travel abroad was far higher in Austin. A 2040 strategic plan was assembled, calling for a doubling over the next twenty years of the airport's current annual passenger count of ten million. A $2.5 billion terminal, runway, and ground-load facilities expansion were approved in 2023 by the city council and are now in the design phase. Greater:SATX has helped implement the more regional approach by creating the Air Service Development Fund, which, like one first established by Opportunity Austin, incentivizes airlines that bring nonstop flights to San Antonio.

Opportunity Austin and greater:SATX are increasingly acting in concert as both pursue a long list of companies exploring relocation or expansion. "I don't think a week goes by where we are not on the phone, talking to one another," Saucedo-Herrera said. "It's a new day."

"One of the benefits of such a strategy is that you can stand together before the legislature like Houston does now and Dallas does now," Farmer said. "House Bill 5 this [2023] session was the holy grail for Opportunity Austin and for greater:SATX. I think the bill is a precursor to what is about to come to the two cities, and I'll add that I am a big admirer of greater:SATX and its CEO Jenna Saucedo-Herrera. Great things will happen in San Antonio too."

The legislation mentioned by Farmer extends the portfolio of tax incentives the state offers companies that relocate to Texas from outside the state, with California the primary target for finding company leaders willing to follow Elon Musk and Tesla to the low-tax, business-friendly state.

"When we started Opportunity Austin, we had no regional collaboration. Round Rock didn't support Georgetown, and Cedar Park didn't support Leander, and so on," Farmer said. He continued,

> The basic tenet when we started was that we were going to work regionally. We were going to try to create that collaborative atmosphere. The way we've approached it is, it's a big intramural game, each and every city in our five-county region. If they have a chance to be the winner of a project, they should put their best foot forward, sharpen their pencil, and make the absolute best proposal. If they get eliminated, they don't start throwing rocks at their neighbor. We've learned that if a project lands in Georgetown, there'll be accretive benefits in San Marcos. So the region benefits. Projecting forward, I would

anticipate that if there is, let's hypothetically say, another car manufacturing facility and it wants to locate somewhere in the megaregion, well, guess what? New Braunfels ought to compete hard for that, and San Marcos and Hutto and Kyle and Seguin and so on. We should compete because we want to have as many great proposals to increase the chance that that company is going to locate here. Then we all fall in and support and work together to get it done.

The arguments for greater connectedness are powerful. It will take a sustained effort and significant investment by all metro area cities in the emerging megaregion to establish multimodal transit options to address the current congestion that makes travel between San Antonio and Austin so time-consuming and frustrating.

Connectedness makes the cities more appealing for family relocations and job investment. A more regionally oriented workforce becomes more plausible if the cities can work together to reduce single-passenger vehicle traffic, implement advanced bus rapid transit, improve air quality and public health, and renew efforts to explore the establishment of an independent passenger rail line.

The continuing growth of Austin and San Antonio is a certainty, making their convergence into one megaregion an inevitability. Redefining the South and Central Texas horizon as a thirteen-county economic zone, similar in geographic size to the Dallas–Fort Worth metro area, creates a completely new dynamic.

Game On

Attracting More Professional Sports Franchises to the Megaregion

I think it would be foolish for the NFL to pass up an opportunity to have a third team in Texas, specifically in the Austin–San Antonio region. I have had conversations with the mayor of Austin about that. I think it makes all the sense in the world for us to position ourselves as the home of the next Texas NFL team.
—Former San Antonio Mayor Ron Nirenberg

Texas is a sports-loving state. Football tops the many sports rivalries that begin in high school and only intensify at the state's major universities and into the realm of professional rivalries. Sports are deeply embedded in Texas culture. Collegiate sports, especially football, are big business in Texas. In the United States, the three largest and most popular professional sports leagues create intercity rivalries. The three top sports leagues as measured by revenue and audience are the National Football League (NFL), Major League Baseball (MLB), and the National Basketball Association (NBA; see table 11.1), although Major League Soccer (MLS) is now in three Texas cities, including Austin. The Professional Golfers' Association Tour, Ladies Professional Golf Association Tour, and Champions Tour together stage eight tournaments throughout the state. San Antonio hosts the Valero Texas Open, the oldest continually played professional golf tournament in a single city on the tour. The World Golf Championships–Dell

Table 11.1.

Professional sports leagues, 2022 revenues

League	Revenue
NFL	$18.6 billion
NBA	$10.58 billion
MLB	$10.32 billion

Source: League statistics, including ticket and television rights payments.

Note: National Hockey League revenues in 2022 were $5.7 billion, so for the purposes of this analysis, only the leagues with $10 billion or more are listed.

Technologies Match Play at Austin Country Club was played for the last time in March 2023.

Great cities have great professional and/or collegiate sports franchises that enjoy broad and intense fan support, help create a sense of identity, and distinguish life in these metro areas from those cities that lack the same entertainment and economic development opportunities. Young professionals weighing multiple job opportunities in different cities are more likely to be attracted to the city where world-class sports are part of the scene. Cities with great sports traditions are recognized globally for their winning teams and their superstars.

The image of a white Texas Longhorn logo on a burnt-orange shirt or ball cap is universally recognized, as is the Texas Longhorn Marching Band and the team's mascot, Bevo. How big is football at the University of Texas at Austin (UT-Austin)? The Darrell K Royal–Texas Memorial Stadium (DKR–Texas Memorial Stadium) seats 101,119 people, making it the ninth-largest stadium in the world. It's named for the university's most revered football coach, Darrell Royal, who served as head football coach from 1957 to 1976, winning three national championships in 1963, 1969, and 1970. His successor, Fred Akers, held the job from 1977 to 1986, losing at the Cotton Bowl in two national championship games in 1977 and 1983 that marred otherwise perfect seasons. Mack Brown, who held the job from 1998 to 2013, delivered Texas the last of its four total national championships in 2005.

Since then, the team and a sequence of head coaches have strug-gled to return the Longhorns to glory. Meanwhile, the football pro-gram at the University of Texas at San Antonio (UTSA) continues to evolve from its birth in 2011 under nationally recognized head coach Larry Coker, who won a national championship with the Miami Hurricanes in 2001. It is now led by head coach Jeff Traylor, one of the state's widely known high school football coaches for many years before rising through the ranks with assistant coaching gigs at Texas, Southern Methodist University, and then Arkansas before coming to UTSA in 2019. The Roadrunners earned their first national ranking in the 2022–23 season. Hopefully, the UT versus UTSA will grow to be a much-anticipated and competitive rivalry that leads fans by the thousands from one city to travel to the other to cheer on their teams. So far they have met only twice, in 2022 and 2024 games that Texas won. A football program was added to UTSA because then–UTSA President Ricardo Romo had seen what had happened on the West Coast when the University of California (UC) at Berkeley, the UC system's flagship campus, dominated the Pac-12 Conference in the past. Later, the University of California at Los Angeles joined the Pac-12 Conference and garnered even more prominence on the college football landscape than the Cal Golden Bears. Romo believed UTSA could repeat that achievement.

The UT-Austin sports program is known for more than foot-ball. Over the years, Longhorn sports teams have won fifty-six total national championships, forty-seven of them National Col-legiate Athletic Association (NCAA) national championships. Var-sity teams in nine men's sports and eleven women's sports are fielded. Baseball, swimming and diving, golf, and rowing teams have all delivered national championships and produced a number of Olympic medal winners.

While UT football and other teams dominate the conversa-tion and collegiate sports generate massive revenue in Austin, the arrival of Austin FC has clearly demonstrated professional soccer can bring the same intense fan support. Q2 Stadium in North Aus-tin, which seats 20,738, opened in 2021. The season-ticket waiting list has risen to 26,000 people. The team has a middling record, but that hasn't stopped the city from embracing the sport or the players. The growth of men's and women's professional soccer in the United States is so strong that earlier in 2023, Egyptian billionaire Mohamed Mansour agreed to pay a record $500 million fee for an expansion franchise in San Diego. Austin embraced its professional soccer franchise much as San Antonio did its professional basketball team five decades earlier. In May 2024, the website Sportico published a ranking of soccer club valuations around the world. Austin FC's $800 million valuation in its fourth season, after an initial $100 million investment, placed the team as the sixth most valuable in the MLS and twenty-first in the world. That is despite Austin FC's smallish stadium. Cities know that collegiate and pro sports franchises not only provide a highly sought-after fan experience for locals. They also serve as marketing arms for the cities to attract talented workers and new residents.

Great coaches and great players in the age of social media become instantly recognizable around the world and associated with the cities where their teams are located. They bring positive publicity to the cities where they play and serve as an effective marketing and promotional arm of the city. Spurs coach Gregg Popovich, David Robinson, and Tim Duncan, all Hall of Fame inductees, get asked for autographs in any airport in any city where they dare venture. Tony Parker in France and Manu Ginóbili in Argentina attract mobs of fans whenever they are spotted returning to their home countries. Spurs executives hope their latest number-one draft pick, France's Victor Wembanyama, will bring the same global attention and fan devotion to San Antonio's five-time NBA champions. The franchise is planning to stage a game in Paris in the 2024–25 season. Boosters hope the arrival of "Wemby" and the ensuing community excitement will lead to a new publicly funded downtown arena, which these days can cost more than $1 billion. Austin and San Antonio have evolved as sports markets differently, and each is working to grow the presence of collegiate and professional sports.

The three leading professional sports leagues have a total of ninety-two franchises, thirty-two in the NFL and thirty each in MLB and the NBA. The MLS has three of its twenty-nine franchises in Texas, one in Houston, Dallas, and now Austin. San Antonio's

The Major League Soccer team Austin FC plays a match against Montreal FC at Austin's Q2 Stadium, March 4, 2023. Photo by Cesar's iPhoneography (Flickr, CC BY-NC-SA).

efforts to attract a franchise have not been successful. Some metro areas and regions are represented by teams in all three sports. Austin–San Antonio is the largest urban area in the country without an NFL or MLB team.

The adjoining Austin–San Antonio metros, which together have a greater population than each of twenty-six states, own only two professional sports franchises, the San Antonio Spurs of the NBA and, as of 2021, Austin FC of MLS, an expansion franchise San Antonio very much coveted and worked without success to win.

Spurs Sports & Entertainment, the City of San Antonio, and Bexar County worked unsuccessfully in 2018 and 2019 to bring an MLS expansion franchise to San Antonio to elevate the existing San Antonio FC team that competes in the second-tier United Soccer League. It was later learned that J. Anthony Precourt Jr., the owner of the MLS's Columbus Crew, was quietly negotiating with Austin to move his team there, which backfired badly with

San Antonio Spurs player Victor Wembanyama from France won the NBA Kia Rookie of the Year award for the 2023–24 season. Photo by Reginald Thomas II. Courtesy of the San Antonio Spurs.

Columbus fans and league executives. Precourt was eventually forced to sell the team to new owners who committed to keeping the Crew in Columbus. The MLS then awarded an expansion franchise to Austin, infuriating San Antonio elected leaders who charged the MLS with negotiating in bad faith. An MLS official had previously stated that only one franchise would be granted and that if Austin was selected, San Antonio would no longer be under consideration.

San Antonio boosters have turned south to work with contacts in Liga MX, formerly known as la Primera División de México in the Mexican Football Federation, in a long-shot hope of winning an expansion team in San Antonio, or more realistically, one or more league matches played annually in the Alamodome, supplanting the periodic exhibition matches now staged by visiting teams.

San Antonio becoming home to a basketball team that would be renamed the Spurs happened by serendipity, although it would not have happened had the city not constructed the HemisFair Arena as part of the HemisFair '68 world's fair. The Dallas franchise was part of the American Basketball Association (ABA), the upstart league challenging the NBA's monopoly. The ABA introduced important changes to the sport, including the three-point shot and the slam-dunk contest at its All-Star Game, but it failed to win television contracts and struggled to stay viable.

The Dallas franchise, known as the Chaparrals, was struggling with poor attendance for several years before a group from San Antonio acquired the team in 1973 and renamed it the Spurs. One of the investors was the late B. J. "Red" McCombs, the larger-than-life owner of a network of auto dealerships, whose hometown was Spur, Texas. McCombs and other investors were especially fortunate when in 1976 four of the ABA teams were welcomed into the NBA and the secondary league ceased to exist. In other words, the NBA never selected San Antonio for a franchise and never likely would have on its own. The value of the Spurs franchise doubled the day it became an NBA franchise.

McCombs and business partner Angelo Drossos's initial acquisition of the Chaparrals was transacted for one dollar, the price of a one-year loan of the team with a three-year option to buy. While the Chaparrals were lucky to draw a few hundred fans in Dallas and an effort to play games in Fort Worth was a bust, the Spurs under McCombs and Drossos drew strong attendance to its initial games at HemisFair Arena. McCombs and Drossos are said to have torn up the option and immediately settled on an undisclosed sales price.

These days, professional sports games are broadcast and live streamed around the world as television networks compete for broadcast and online content that generates once unimaginable advertising revenue. Individual players make more money in a few seasons than entire franchises were worth only a few decades ago. Franchise values have risen exponentially, and their value to cities is far beyond economic metrics. Of the ninety-two franchises in the three leading sports in the United States, Texas has seven (see table 11.2). The state has two NFL franchises (the Dallas Cowboys and the Houston Texans), two MLB teams (the Texas Rangers and the Houston Astros), three NBA teams (the Dallas Mavericks, the Houston Rockets, and the San Antonio Spurs), and three MLS teams (the Houston Dynamo FC, FC Dallas, and Austin FC).

The New York region, the nation's largest metro, has six of the ninety-two professional sports franchises in the nation, two each in the NFL (the Giants and the Jets), MLB (the Yankees and the Mets), and the NBA (the Knicks and the Brooklyn Nets). As the nation's second-largest metro, Los Angeles also has six of the ninety-two franchises, two each in the NFL (the Rams and the Chargers), MLB (the Dodgers and the Angels), and the NBA (the Lakers and the Clippers). Chicago, the nation's third-largest metro, has four

Table 11.2.

Sports franchises in top states

State	Total	NFL	MLB	NBA
California	12	3	5	4
Florida	8	3	3	2
New York	7	3	2	2
Texas	7	2	2	3

Source: Author compilation.

franchises, the Bears in the NFL, the White Sox and the Cubs in MLB, and the Bulls in the NBA.

The nine largest metros each have at least one team in all three professional leagues—New York, Los Angeles, Chicago, Dallas, Houston, Washington, Philadelphia, Atlanta, and Miami. Austin–San Antonio would be the tenth-largest US metro if it were considered as one market.

Six metros that have teams in the three leagues are smaller than Austin and San Antonio combined. They are Minnesota, Boston, Phoenix, Detroit, Cleveland, and Denver. San Francisco, the seventh city that is home to three franchises, has less population than San Antonio, but the Bay Area teams consider the population in San Jose, a separate metro area, as being part of the San Francisco sports market. If San Francisco's metro and San Jose's metro were combined, it would be larger than Austin–San Antonio.

Six other cities have professional teams in two of the leagues despite having smaller metropolitan areas than Austin–San Antonio. They are Charlotte (the NFL's Carolina Panthers and the NBA's Hornets), Pittsburgh (the NFL's Steelers and MLB's Pirates), Kansas City (the NFL's Chiefs and MLB's Royals), Milwaukee (the NBA's Bucks and MLB's Brewers), Indianapolis (the NFL's Colts and the NBA's Pacers), and New Orleans (the NFL's Saints and the NBA's Pelicans). In short, Austin–San Antonio is the largest urban area without multiple professional sports franchises from the three largest leagues.

By this analysis, Texas and especially Austin–San Antonio are therefore underrepresented among the three leagues despite the fact that Texas has the nation's second-largest population. As mentioned earlier, Austin–San Antonio's five million people is greater than the entire population in the neighboring state of Louisiana. Yet Louisiana has the NFL's New Orleans Saints and the NBA's New Orleans Pelicans. Quite a few other aforementioned NFL cities have smaller markets than Austin–San Antonio.

Why? Several reasons can be cited. Especially in the NFL and MLB, franchises date back to decades when their host cities were ranked higher in population, before the Austin and San Antonio populations began to grow at record rates. Although leagues have undergone franchise expansions over the decades, team conferences and divisions formed in ways that made geographic sense.

When leagues expanded the number of franchises, officials often looked at a metro's corporate community as a sign of business wealth and of the general incomes of the population. This was important to gauge the markets for purchases of luxury boxes, ticket sales, and other revenue streams for franchise owners. Austin–San Antonio has a disadvantage in this. Dallas and Houston each are corporate headquarters for more than twenty Fortune 500 companies. Austin–San Antonio is home to five, although the area is dotted with numerous privately owned large companies.

Another factor is that franchise owners are reluctant to provide funding for stadiums themselves, putting the burden on cities and states to underwrite the building of league-standard stadiums. Stadiums are becoming more expensive to build because of the rising costs of land, construction materials, and labor. Plus, league standards periodically are raised to force more amenities, especially lucrative luxury boxes. The Cowboys' eighty-thousand-seat AT&T Stadium, which opened in 2009, cost $1.2 billion. Allegiant Stadium, the Raiders' new sixty-five-thousand-seat stadium in Las Vegas, opened in 2020 and cost $1.9 billion. Compare those numbers to San Antonio's sixty-four-thousand-seat Alamodome, which opened in 1993 and cost $186 million.

The largest existing sports stadium in Austin–San Antonio is UT's DKR–Texas Memorial Stadium, home field for the UT Longhorns. The initial small version of the field was built in the 1920s and paid out of student fees. Several phases of expansion have been financed by wealthy alumni. DKR–Texas Memorial can accommodate crowds of more than one hundred thousand people, but it would not meet strict NFL standards now, especially in some of the concession corridors.

San Antonio was the largest city in the nation without a professional sports–sized stadium until 1993 when the Alamodome opened. The Alamodome has a capacity of about sixty-five thousand for football. It was built at an initial cost of $186 million with revenues from a portion of city sales tax revenues collected for five years. The Alamodome was built with the hope of attracting an NFL franchise, either as an expansion team or as a franchise relocation. Several strong courtships ensued: the New Orleans Saints; the Minnesota Vikings, then owned by McCombs; and the Oakland Raiders before committing to Las Vegas.

The Alamodome now is the home field of the Division One UTSA Roadrunners football team, which finished as champions of the Conference USA in 2021 and 2022 and has now moved to the American Athletic Conference. The Alamodome also hosts the annual Alamo Bowl football game staged at the end of December. Like most other college football bowls, the Alamo Bowl was established to fill vacant hotel rooms in December and early January when convention bookings and activities take a break, in addition to the community pride in being host to a bowl game. The Alamo Bowl and the Alamodome have done that. The Alamodome continues to receive millions of dollars' worth of upgrades to remain in the running for men's and women's NCAA Final Four basketball championship games periodically. The NCAA Final Four men's championships have occurred in 1998, 2004, 2008, and 2018 and will return in 2025. The NCAA women's Final Four championships occurred in 2002, 2010, and 2021 and will return in 2029.

The Alamodome was, for a while, home for the San Antonio Spurs, which won its first NBA championship trophy in 1999 while located there. But the Spurs used less than half of the seating, with a curtain creating an arena within the stadium. The Alamodome's first major event was the US Olympic Festival in 1993. The City of San Antonio later demolished HemisFair Arena, the Spurs' first home, to make way for the expansion of the Henry B. González Convention Center. The Spurs' home court, now named the Frost Center, is a county-owned arena on the city's East Side that needs periodic upgrades to meet rising NBA standards.

It remains unclear whether Austin or San Antonio voters would approve public spending for a new stadium typically sought by NFL owners, for either an expansion team or a relocation. Training facilities are another requirement. Neither Austin nor San Antonio possesses a baseball stadium meeting MLB standards. San Antonio's minor-league team, the Missions, a Double-A affiliate of the San Diego Padres, has been acquired by a new group of local owners seeking to build an upgraded stadium, likely downtown, to meet updated minor-league standards. The owners hope a new stadium earns the team a promotion to Triple-A status. Austin, in its metropolitan neighbor Round Rock, also has a ballpark, home to the Round Rock Express, a Triple-A team affiliated with the Texas Rangers and owned by MLB Hall of Fame pitcher Nolan Ryan.

For a brief time in 2005, following the devastation in New Orleans caused by Hurricane Katrina, the Alamodome was selected to host three of the Saints' home games. Owner Tom Benson had strong business and personal ties to San Antonio as a banker and owner of car dealerships. San Antonio fans and a number of civic leaders hoped to make the move from New Orleans permanent. NFL officials opposed any effort to move the franchise out of heavily damaged New Orleans, and a financial aid deal was brokered with the state of Louisiana to repair the Superdome. Yet the San Antonio area in 2005 was a larger market than New Orleans, which lost significant population after Katrina. In 2021, San Antonio had grown to become the twenty-fourth-largest metropolitan area, while Austin grew to the twenty-sixth largest. New Orleans ranked forty-seventh. The three 2005 Saints games in San Antonio drew an average attendance of 62,665 people, despite San Antonio's strong fan base for the Dallas Cowboys.

In 2017, the Oakland Raiders organization decided it needed a new home because the Oakland Coliseum was aging and had flooding and sewage problems. The Raiders' ownership let it be known that San Antonio was a possible new home. The owners ultimately obtained a publicly financed deal for a new stadium in Las Vegas, brokered by the governor of Nevada. The team became the Las Vegas Raiders in 2020. Again, each of the San Antonio and the Austin metros by themselves is larger than the twenty-ninth-ranked Las Vegas metro.

San Antonio's McCombs purchased the NFL's Minnesota Vikings in 1998 for $250 million, thus joining the NFL family. McCombs's aim was to either eventually move the Vikings to San Antonio or leverage his Vikings' ownership to obtain a second franchise that would be in San Antonio. The state of Minnesota, however, created a $200 million penalty if the Vikings were ever moved from the aging Hubert H. Humphrey Metrodome. Leaving the stadium became impractical, and McCombs could not negotiate the construction of a new stadium. He decided in 2005 to sell the Vikings to Zygi Wilf for $625 million, or $375 million more than he had paid for it.

In 2021, the Buffalo Bills saw a need for a new stadium and suggested it may have to leave New York, possibly for Austin or between Austin and San Antonio. Political leadership in Buffalo and Albany came up with a funding plan for a replacement stadium in Buffalo, the nation's forty-ninth-ranked metro. In each of these three examples, the qualifications for Austin–San Antonio to support major league sports were evident, enough at least to be used to secure public stadium financing.

Another hurdle for Austin–San Antonio to attract an NFL franchise is team owners, who must approve expansion teams and their cities. It will be difficult to get past the influential Dallas Cowboys owner, billionaire Jerry Jones, who many people believe opposes a third NFL franchise for Texas because it would shrink the television market for the Cowboys, reducing advertising and merchandising revenues. NFL Commissioner Roger Goodell could initiate an NFL expansion effort, but he answers to the owners, and Jones is arguably the most powerful owner. Austin–San Antonio television viewers, not to mention those farther south in Mexico, have long been a loyal and lucrative fan base for Jones. Word around the newsroom of the *San Antonio Express-News* in the 1970s and 1980s was that when the Dallas Cowboys were playing on television, the police radio monitored by reporters would go silent. Auto traffic was reduced to the point that few collisions were reported. In the 1990s, one Federal Reserve Bank of Dallas economist assigned to San Antonio joked that San Antonio most assuredly had an NFL team—the Cowboys—and the great thing was, residents didn't even have to pay for a stadium to have its franchise.

"I think it would be foolish for the NFL to pass up an opportunity to have a third team in Texas, specifically in the Austin–San Antonio region," said former San Antonio Mayor Ron Nirenberg. "I have had conversations with the mayor of Austin about that. I think it makes all the sense in the world for us to position ourselves as the home of the next Texas NFL team."

In favor of major professional sports expansion in Austin and San Antonio is the success of the San Antonio Spurs. The Spurs celebrated their fiftieth anniversary in the city in January 2023 with a special regular-season game staged at the Alamodome, the team's previous home. For the game, the whole stadium was opened instead of half of the Alamodome. The game drew 68,323 fans, smashing the previous NBA regular-season single-game record, a sign of how it draws residents together. The Spurs lost the game to the Golden State Warriors. It didn't matter because the fans were there to celebrate a half century of Spurs and community success.

"I think the Spurs, if you look at their history and see what they have accomplished in San Antonio, are representative of what can happen with other franchises that come into this area," said retired MLB star pitcher Nolan Ryan.

The key will be to form ownership groups poised to pounce on any franchise opportunity that arises.

"If [MLB] gets to the mindset where they are thinking about expansion, an effort will have to be organized here in Central Texas to get an ownership group together willing to make that commitment and take it to Major League Baseball," Ryan said, adding,

> What we are going to see is that San Antonio and Austin are going to be a metroplex like Dallas and Fort Worth, and I expect it to be the same way. That ballpark up in Arlington [the Texas Rangers' Globe Life Field] sits between the two of them. I think [Austin–San Antonio] is going to be an opportunity for professional sports to look at this area and see the attractiveness of it and where they might want to move and locate. . . . I think [the NFL] will look at this area. It's an opportunity for them to move into a strong market.

MLB, which currently has thirty teams, plans to expand to thirty-two franchises at some future date. Uncertainties arose in early 2024 over a pending move by the Oakland Athletics to Las

Vegas, but the move then became solid. While that move was still sketchy, however, ESPN published an article that listed Austin–San Antonio as the number-one alternative and labeled Austin as the most likely site for a stadium, even suggesting a nickname of the Austin Bats. Local commentators, however, said an Austin suburb, such as Round Rock, would be more likely to pay for all or a part of a stadium, which an ownership group would prefer. Commentators also cited the trend of owners relying heavily on the sale of stadium luxury boxes for profits, pointing to Austin as the best-positioned city for patrons to buy luxury boxes. A stadium south of Austin, between Austin and San Antonio, remains a remote possibility. Other possible expansion or relocation MLB cities listed by ESPN include Charlotte, North Carolina, and Mexico City. Other sources speculate that possible MLB franchises could include Nashville, Salt Lake City, Portland, and Sacramento.

Meanwhile, the Spurs organization has based its development team, the Austin Spurs, in Austin. In the 2022–23 and 2023–24 seasons, the Spurs played several regular-season games in Austin's new Moody Center on the UT campus. More games will be scheduled in Austin, Mexico City, and the Alamodome in the future.

"The underlying logic to that is that the organization has a lot of foresight. They are trying to capture the market from Austin all the way down to Mexico City to let those fans know, 'Hey, we recognize you. We see you,'" said Sean Elliott, former Spurs forward and two-time NBA All-Star. "We do have a lot of season-ticket holders who drive down from Austin to come to games. I think Spurs fans should be secure. The Spurs are not going anywhere. We're just trying to capture that market. We're not trying to move. We're just trying to engage that fan base a lot more." Elliott, an on-air analyst for Spurs games, is best remembered for the Memorial Day Miracle, a last-second three-point shot in the Alamodome against the Portland Trailblazers in the 1999 Western Conference Finals. That unforgettable moment propelled the Spurs forward to their first NBA championship, defeating the New York Knicks, four games to one, in the finals.

The Spurs organization watches urban economic measures closely.

"There's a paradox; the burgeoning and growing population of this region that has obviously been going on for twenty years now in a top-ten ranking continuously is one of the interesting data points," said Peter J. Holt, Spurs Sports & Entertainment chairman. He continued,

It's real, however, there are especially some economic indexes [that] aren't tracking in the same way. As we see population growth really explode, there isn't exactly the same tracking of economic indexes. If you look at household income, if you look at educational attainment, if you look at median salaries compared to our Texas relatives and national relatives, if you look at housing growth and educational outcomes at all levels, they are not tracking in the same [direction] as the core population. If you really looked at corporate headquarters, such as Fortune 500, if you look at these tracking, correlating datasets, they are not exactly aligned. Some of that is a significant contributor to the overall opportunity that not just a sports franchise looks at but media entertainment venues. Everyone in this consumer world is going to look at these indexes and say, "What's the headline opportunity?"

Holt added,

If it was just population, there probably would be more of a mirror to other markets because [however] you scrape the data around, we could be looked at as a top-ten population metro or region in the US. If we are in the top ten, why don't we have multiple sports franchises? You really have to dig into a lot of the economic indexes to see, is the opportunity viable? My gut answer is that yes, in my lifetime, there will be more. My more nuanced, realistic answer is, I don't know. The reason for the "I don't know" is demographics and the changing dynamics of professional sports franchises and sports leagues. The dynamics of the leagues, the dynamics of the individual cities in the region, and just consumer dynamics and wealth indices will contribute to that decision.

It would help aid in what ultimately will be a cultural goal coming to fruition, which would be a sense of community and identity, having residents in San Antonio and Austin and in between [to have] a regional identity as opposed to just "I'm an Austin resident, and I do things in San Antonio" and vice versa. There's no better way to do that than a sports affiliation. Having that sense of community identity throughout a region that would support a professional team, like a third NFL team, would be a boon for development in the corridor.

—Former San Antonio Mayor Ron Nirenberg

San Antonio has proved to the NBA that the city and the region can and do support professional sports, no matter what the other two leagues believe. Helping this has been the Spurs' athletic success on the court. The Spurs have won five NBA championships—1999, 2003, 2005, 2007, and 2014. People in the Austin–San Antonio megaregion are waiting for the day when the football and baseball professional leagues wake up to the opportunity here. It will help if potential owners in Austin and San Antonio form partnerships that are ready when that day comes.

Another step forward would be realized if a regional sports financing and bonding authority were created. Local government officials and business leaders could be appointed to an organization that would be ready with answers to questions from leagues and investors on the options for land and possible public financing by the municipalities, either individual cities or a mixture of them, in the megaregion. Such an authority, which might require state legislation, could give the Austin–San Antonio megaregion a head start when existing franchises seek new homes or new franchise opportunities arise.

Professional sports stadiums may be built, operated, and upgraded in several ways. A sports bond-financing authority, sometimes involving a local sales tax, is one option. Ownership by a state, county, or city is another option. States and counties can be vital for regional stadiums built outside of core cities in the franchise's market. Examples exist, too, of an owner or ownership group of a franchise to finance, own, and operate a stadium without public involvement.

One example of a sports bond-financing authority is Arrowhead Stadium, home of the NFL's Kansas City Chiefs. The franchise originated in Dallas as the Dallas Texans of the now defunct American Football League. The franchise moved to Kansas City in 1963 and originally played home games at the 1923-built Municipal Stadium, shared with the MLB team. The Chiefs organization was unable to find a suitable stadium site within Kansas City city limits, but Jackson County, which is in the Kansas City metropolitan area, offered to issue a $102 million bond package that was approved by county voters in 1967. Ground was broken in 1968 outside of Kansas City and southwest of Independence, Missouri, the Jackson County seat (see table 11.3). Two stadiums: one for the Chiefs football team and another for the Kansas City Royals, the MLB franchise that began in 1969 after the Kansas City Athletics moved to Oakland in 1967. That was the beginning of the Truman Sports Complex, owned and operated by the Jackson County Sports Complex Authority. Arrowhead Stadium opened more than fifty years ago, in 1972, and is now named GEHA Field at Arrowhead Stadium. The complex also is the site of the Royals' Kauffman Stadium. The Jackson County Sports Complex Authority conducted a $375 million upgrade of Arrowhead in 2010 and in 2024 was seeking a new sales tax authorization from Jackson County voters for another round of improvements.

The Arizona Sports & Tourism Authority owns State Farm Stadium in Glendale, Arizona, the home of the NFL's Arizona Cardinals. Glendale is a municipality in the Phoenix metropolitan area. The facility was called the University of Phoenix Stadium from 2006 to 2018 and is the replacement of the previous Cardinals' home, Sun Devil Stadium in Tempe. State Farm Stadium also has been the site of the Phoenix area's Fiesta Bowl college postseason football game since 2007. When the Cardinals held games in Tempe, in Arizona State University's stadium, several Phoenix-area cities bid to build a new NFL-standard stadium. The decision was to be made by the

Table 11.3.

Sample of regional stadiums outside of the city the franchises represent

Stadium	Team	Location
GEHA Field at Arrowhead Stadium	Kansas City Chiefs	Kansas City, Missouri
State Farm Stadium	Arizona Cardinals	Glendale, Arizona
Levi's Stadium	San Francisco 49ers	Santa Clara, California
Highmark Stadium	Buffalo Bills	Orchard Park, New York
AT&T Stadium	Dallas Cowboys	Arlington, Texas
MetLife Stadium	New York Jets and New York Giants	East Rutherford, New Jersey
Hard Rock Stadium	Miami Dolphins	Miami Gardens, Florida
Gillette Stadium	New England Patriots	Foxborough, Massachusetts
Commanders Field	Washington Commanders	Prince George's County, Maryland
SoFi Stadium	Los Angeles Rams and Los Angeles Chargers	Inglewood, California

Arizona Tourism & Sports Authority, created by voter approval in 2000. Tempe and Avondale were early front-runners. Later, Mesa and Glendale placed bids. Glendale became the choice after Mesa voters did not approve the stadium. Construction costing $455 million began in 2003, and the stadium opened in 2006. The bonds are financed by event revenues, hotel car rental taxes, and sales tax revenues. The Arizona Cardinals contributed $143 million, and the City of Glendale added $9.5 million. Renovations followed in 2014 and 2017.

The Santa Clara Stadium Authority owns the home of the San Francisco 49ers, Levi's Stadium. The stadium sits about forty miles south of San Francisco, in the city of Santa Clara, a smaller community next door to the larger city of San Jose. In 2006, the

NFL franchise 49ers proposed a new stadium to replace the aging Candlestick Park. Talks with the City of San Francisco failed to reach any agreement, so the franchise turned its attention to Santa Clara, where the team already operated an administrative and training center. Construction began in 2012 with a loan from private investors. The NFL itself lent $200 million to the project. The $1.3 billion stadium opened in 2014. The owner, the Santa Clara Stadium Authority, finances the stadium through naming rights, corporate sponsorships, personal seat licenses, ticket surcharges, and the lease by the 49ers franchise. Santa Clara voters approved tax-exempt status for the Santa Clara Stadium Authority, and the city leases the stadium site to the authority.

Cities, counties, and states build and own other stadiums. The state of New York will be the owner of the planned home stadium for the Buffalo Bills when it is scheduled for completion in 2026. Now, during construction, the stadium is called the New Highmark Stadium. Upon completion, it will be called Highmark Stadium, replacing the current stadium next door in Orchard Park, New York, outside of Buffalo. The current stadium, owned by Erie County, will be demolished. In 2014, then-Gov. Andrew Cuomo appointed a study board to produce plans for a new stadium. Months later, Bills owner Ralph Wilson died. Planning continued, with new owners Terry and Kim Pegula joining the study group. Planning stalled. The Pegulas in 2021 demanded a new $1.1 billion Orchard Park stadium be built at taxpayer expense or else the franchise would seek a new home. Austin was mentioned by the franchise as a possibility, which was a surprise in Austin because no one had contacted the city. The matter was settled in 2022 with an agreement on a $1.4 billion stadium in Orchard Park. New York State is scheduled to pay $600 million, Erie County $250 million, and the Bills $350 million, with the NFL lending $200 million. A $300 million cost increase announced in 2023 will be covered by the Bills.

The City of Arlington, Texas, between Dallas and Fort Worth, owns AT&T Stadium, which is operated by the Dallas Cowboys. The $1.15 billion stadium was built from 2006 to 2009 after Arlington voters approved a half-cent sales tax increase and the devotion of hotel occupancy and car rental taxes to the project. The City of Arlington itself added $325 million in bonds. Cowboys owner Jerry Jones agreed to pay for any cost overruns. The NFL lent $150 million. The Jones family has privately placed about $150 million for enhancements in the stadium since its opening, a figure that will rise to $500 million by 2025. Many other events are held there each year, including the Big 12 football championship game and the Cotton Bowl Classic bowl game. AT&T Stadium replaced Texas Stadium in Irving, the home of the Cowboys from 1971 to 2008.

The NFL's New York Jets and the New York Giants came together in 1998 to form the New Meadowlands Stadium Company, now MetLife Stadium Co., to build and own a new joint home stadium, MetLife Stadium, in East Rutherford, New Jersey. MetLife Stadium sits in the Meadowlands Sports Complex. The complex itself is owned and operated by the New Jersey Sports and Exposition Authority, which was created by the New Jersey Legislature in 1971 in an attempt at providing New York professional sports teams with new stadiums. The $1.6 billion MetLife Stadium, opened in 2010, sits next door to the site of the stadium it replaced, the now demolished Giants Stadium. The Jets originally wanted a stadium in Manhattan on the Lower West Side, but the idea died partly because of its requirement for public funding. MetLife can be converted for use from one team to the other team in a matter of hours. Each team has its own permanent locker room, with two other locker rooms used by visiting teams. Helping MetLife Stadium Co. is parking revenue from part of MetLife's parking lot year round when other events are held at the Meadowlands.

Two other NFL stadiums that have been privately built are in the Miami and Boston areas. The Hard Rock Stadium in Miami Gardens, Florida, in Miami-Dade County, is home to the NFL's Miami Dolphins. The stadium is shared with the University of Miami Hurricanes football team. Hard Rock Stadium opened in 1987 as a replacement for Miami's old Orange Bowl. Team founder Joe Robbie decided to build the new stadium when the City of Miami in 1976 quadrupled the rent of the Orange Bowl. Hard Rock

Stadium was built for both football and baseball and for a period was home to the MLB Florida Marlins team. Gillette Stadium is another regional stadium, in Foxborough, Massachusetts, twenty-two miles from Boston. It is the home for the NFL's New England Patriots. The $325 million stadium was built between 2000 and 2002 by Patriots owner Robert Kraft and his company, the Kraft Group. Gillette Stadium is the replacement for the previous Foxboro Stadium. The need for a new Patriots stadium became apparent in 1984, and the prolonged search for a site included two places in Boston, one of them next to baseball's famed Fenway Park, home of the Red Sox, and sites in Hartford, Connecticut, and Providence, Rhode Island.

One of these options—a regional sports bonding authority, city or county ownership, or private ownership—will be necessary should the Austin–San Antonio megaregion become the focus for a new NFL or MLB franchise or the relocation of an existing one from elsewhere. They are all proven models. The NFL will not select a new franchise site unless a plan is in place. A sports bonding authority would not have to spend any money until a franchise is secured. But the bonding authority can identify land and site options before the land becomes too expensive. If a regional sports bonding authority is created by state legislation and based in a city or county and then is paired with a ready ownership group, the people of the Austin–San Antonio megaregion could embrace a new professional sports franchise.

12

The Future of the
Austin–San Antonio Megaregion

I believe the lines between our cities are going to blur with respect to the kinds of bigger services we provide, whether that is air service or any kind of entertainment amenities. I think people will start to feel like it's Austin–San Antonio, as opposed to "I live in San Antonio, and I am going to be in San Antonio, and I am going to rely on San Antonio for all my needs" or vice versa in Austin.

—Former San Antonio Mayor Ron Nirenberg

If you listen to the demographers, we have a lot of work to do. We are going to have to be very mindful and very intentional about what we do, not only with roadways and rail, but with water, energy, and housing. That said, I am a believer that our best days are ahead of us.

—Gary Farmer, founder of Opportunity Austin

The future of the big cities in Texas is easy to see. In a few words, it's unending growth. The challenges and opportunities coming with that record growth are epic in nature and urgent in scope. We cannot simply watch and wait for that growth. The time to act is now. The numbers tell the story.

Myths aside, the majority of Texans have lived in the state's urban areas for more than fifty years, and the growth trends all point to its big cities getting even bigger. The Austin and San Antonio metro areas are growing the fastest of all, and with ample land

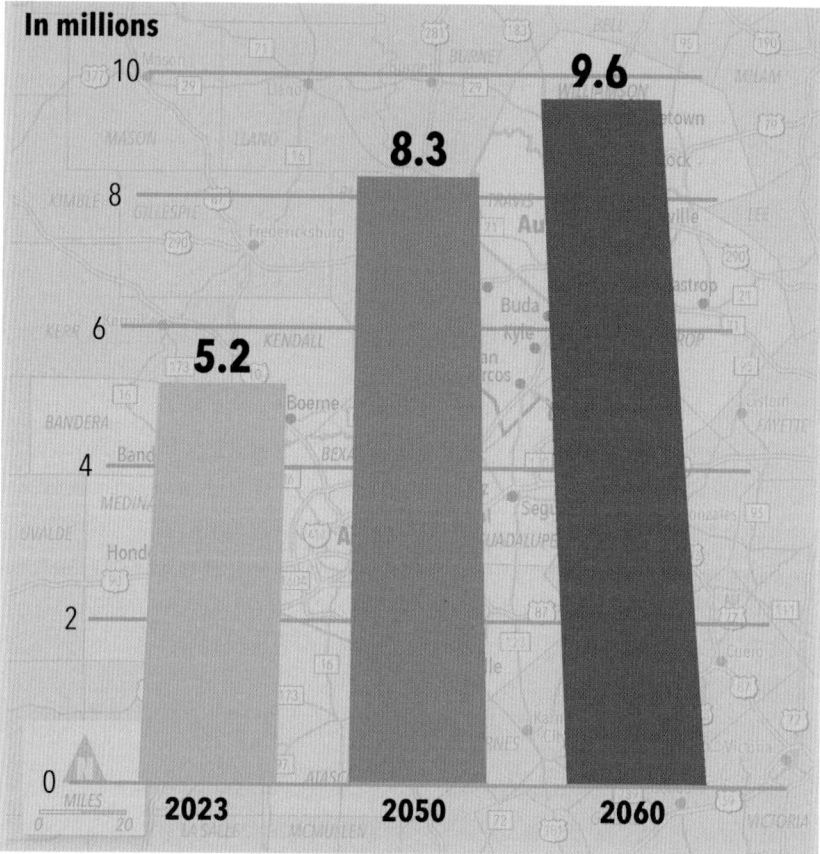

Population projections for the 13 counties of the Austin–San Antonio Metropolitan statistical areas: Texas Demographic Center projections for 13 counties add up to larger steps in population rise in the coming decades, based on population growth in recent years. Graphic by Mike Fisher.

for expansion and with so many corridor cities thriving, it's easy to see why demographers have already concluded that Austin and San Antonio, once two cities so very different and so dissimilar, are now on their way to becoming a single, interdependent megaregion.

The two metros are each on a path to become home to more than four million people by mid-century. The Austin metropolitan area population was 2.47 million people in 2023. It will grow to 4.37 million in 2050, according to the Texas Demographic Center (TDC). The San Antonio metro area population reached 2.7 million in 2023.

That will grow to 3.93 million people in 2050, about 440,000 people fewer than the Austin metro the same year. The robust growth in the corridor and surrounding cities is what will make Austin–San Antonio a single megaregion by 2050, when the combined population, now 5.18 million, will be 8.3 million. That's more than the present-day Dallas–Fort Worth (DFW) or Houston metros. Raw population projections from the TDC for the thirteen counties in the two metros add up to 9.6 million people by 2060.

Such growth does, indeed, create enormous opportunities and challenges. The attractions are evident: Even with the cost of living rising in both cities, Austin and San Antonio remain attractive destinations for companies and individuals now based on the East and West Coasts where taxes are higher, open land is scarce, and the cost of housing, in particular, continues to drive people into the Sunbelt.

Growth patterns, however, must be managed and not allowed to sprawl haphazardly. At present, the Austin–San Antonio corridor, from Pflugerville to Floresville, with all the suburbs in between,

Although the grocery chain H-E-B has its headquarters in San Antonio, the company placed its futuristic Eastside Tech Hub in Austin to handle its digital operations. The site also is the headquarters for Favor, H-E-B's delivery subsidiary. Photo by Al Rendon.

Visitors enjoy the gaming and esports room at the Boeing Center at Tech Port built inside Port San Antonio, a business park at the former site of Kelly Air Force Base. The Boeing Center also features food and concert halls. Photo by Al Rendon.

is narrowly developed along I-35. The corridor will widen east and west away from I-35 because of the availability of undeveloped land. The targets for growth to the east of the interstate are smaller cities, including Bastrop, Lockhart, Luling, and Seguin. New housing subdivisions are under construction near Lockhart in Caldwell County. New manufacturing is slated for Seguin. To the west, Dripping Springs and Boerne are already growth hot spots with great schools, low crime rates, and rich amenities even as they retain a small-town feel. They offer easy access to the Texas Hill Country. Land is available, even plentiful, for this widening of the corridor, although care must be taken to maintain the area's environmental treasures with controlled, responsible growth. As growth spreads away from I-35, the thirteen-county Austin–San

Antonio megaregion will look less like a linear corridor and will more likely resemble the spread clusters of other US megaregions.

Responsible land-use and environmental policies are only two of the challenges that a fast-growing region such as Austin–San Antonio must address. One can study the development errors and leadership oversights that can trip up regions that once enjoyed moments of economic preeminence and yet faded into the shadows. Some metros faded after failing to anticipate the transition to the next iteration of the industry sectors that fueled their prosperity; others because the very scale of their success created resource problems they didn't foresee. History has not been kind to other urban areas that were the hot megaregions of their time but failed to create sustainable trajectories. There is no guarantee that urban growth will continue indefinitely if solutions to the most pressing problems are not achieved.

The twentieth century saw the rise and fall of multiple cities and regions:

New England

New England was the textile and industrial capital of the country for two centuries. Cities such as Manchester, New Hampshire; Lowell, Massachusetts; and Rochester, Syracuse, and Buffalo, New York, were each the focal points of entire national economic sectors. It was the foundries and machine shops of these cities that equipped the Union armies in the Civil War with the armaments that outmatched the weapons of the agricultural South. In time, many of those factories were overtaken by new technologies, and in other cases, entire industries migrated to other regions, including the American South. Job losses led to economic collapse in many manufacturing towns, resulting in massive population displacement.

Some cities have recovered, such as Manchester, which adapted to the technology wave emanating from Boston's I-95 tech clusters. However, the loss of economic function is evident in many New England communities today in the form of dying downtowns, empty buildings, poverty-stricken neighborhoods, and social dysfunction.

Detroit

Detroit was the nation's fourth-largest city in 1920. In the years after World War II, America's auto industry became the most dominant in the world, and the Motor City enjoyed decades of prosperity. Until it didn't. In the 1950s, Detroit had a population of 2 million people; today, it has less than 650,000. Japanese and German car companies won significant market shares of the automotive industry in the 1970s and '80s, catching self-confident US automakers unprepared for the competition. Detroit began to experience massive economic downturns and population flight. Only an unprecedented federal bailout by the Obama administration in 2009 prevented the demise of the city's flagship corporate leader, General Motors. Detroit itself declared bankruptcy in 2013, unable to meet more than $18 billion in obligations. Detroit is now the twenty-ninth-largest city in the nation. It is laboring mightily to restore life to its downtown and attract young professionals and using its professional sports venues to create attractive new residential districts. But the public discourse in Detroit is too often about how to provide public services in a geography characterized by vast areas of abandoned buildings and open spaces with one or two homes remaining from what were once dense and exciting neighborhoods now hollowed out by an exodus of residents.

Pittsburgh

Pittsburgh was once synonymous with the steel industry, the twelfth-largest city in the nation in 1960, with about 700,000 people in its core. Its culture of gritty toughness was evident to a nation that saw the dominance of the six-time National Football League Champion Pittsburgh Steelers mirror the supremacy of the city's red-hot mills and forging plants. That industrial preeminence is long gone; only in recent years has the City of Three Rivers reinvented itself as a technology, health-care, and higher education hub. Today, its population is around 303,000, the sixty-eighth-largest city in the country.

Silicon Valley

Silicon Valley on the peninsula south of San Francisco was wild fields surrounding cattle ranches and farms in the 1800s. By the early years of the twentieth century, it had been organized into fruit orchards that were so productive that the area was known as the Valley of Heart's Delight. In the intervening years, epic events transformed the region into a global center for high technology and innovation. The Bay Area became a focal point for US Navy research, which accelerated at Moffett Field in the postwar years. In the same period, clusters of inventors and engineers gathered around Stanford University. By the late 1950s and '60s, breakout innovations were fueling the growth of Hewlett-Packard, Shockley Semiconductor Laboratory, Fairchild, Intel, and the Defense Department's ARPANET, predecessor to the Internet. Venture capital firms developed along Sand Hill Road, and Silicon Valley became synonymous with the computer culture, software systems, semiconductor advances, and Internet applications. Today, the San Francisco Bay Area has the largest concentration of high-tech firms, the highest concentration of high-tech jobs, and the highest average high-tech salaries in the United States. But the region's unprecedented growth has unleashed unanticipated problems that threaten its momentum. Silicon Valley faces a severe housing shortage emerging from the imbalance between new jobs and housing starts. By the mid-2010s, the Financial Post labeled Silicon Valley the most expensive housing locale in the nation. The accelerating high cost of living set in motion a spiral of unaffordability, difficulty in retaining young professionals, decentralization of company operations to other locations, and start-up entrepreneurs departing for Salt Lake City, Denver, Austin, and other cities offering affordability, attractive lifestyles, and strong start-up cultures. Traffic congestion and the costs of transportation from distant affordable locations are among the shortfalls in infrastructure that present public leaders with a Gordian knot of implacable challenges. Silicon Valley is a wealthy, productive, and globally significant economic engine, but it is also an objective lesson in preparing in advance for the effects of long-term cumulative growth.

San Francisco is a city suffering from its own prior success and now faces unprecedented homelessness, street crime, and vacant offices once home to businesses that have packed up and departed.

. . .

No one is saying that Austin and San Antonio are candidates for economic collapse. But the region could find itself unable to solve worsening problems associated with unmanaged growth that place the region's economic momentum at risk.

What would failure to prepare for growth look like? The following imaginary excerpts of online stories from the *San Antonio Express-News* and the *Austin American-Statesman* dated August 1, 2030, only five years from now, paint the picture of what failure could look like:

Because transportation leaders failed to add adequate capacity to existing roadways and have not completed significant mass transit projects across the region, traffic gridlock has become so severe that it seriously hinders mobility. Congestion actually reinforces the separation of communities and gives the lie to assertions of a cohesive region. It causes business productivity losses directly attributable to travel times that have become unpredictable and excessive.

A workable balance has not been achieved between older fossil-fuel electric-generating plants and large-scale renewable power, resulting in air-quality restrictions with implications for industrial permitting. Additionally, hopes for the deployment of electric vehicles on a scale that would significantly reduce vehicular emissions have been hampered by the reality of insufficient power in the unstable and unpredictable regional grid.

Strict mandatory water conservation requirements have become necessary as recurrent droughts and water overuse have reduced reliance on the Highland Lakes and the overdrafting of groundwater has damaged water quality in the area's aquifers, resulting in intermittent suspensions of residential building permits across the region.

Housing prices have risen annually by double-digit increments as residential construction has been stalled due to water and power permitting restrictions. Young professionals victimized by the shortages in the housing supply are forced to seek employment in the newer emerging technology cities in parts of the nation that can offer less expensive housing.

Companies that had relocated to the region in the early 2020s and companies that once had plans to locate facilities in the Austin–San Antonio region are following the young talent, the water permits, the housing starts, and the power reserves to other areas.

Uneven educational outcomes across the region's K-12 schools have made it impossible to create a pool of tech-ready graduates of sufficient size to match the demand for workers. Additionally, low school performance scores impede the path to higher education and are forcing new economy companies to look elsewhere to fill their workforce needs. That leaves local students in lower-wage jobs and pushes both poverty levels and social tensions higher. The region's new minority-majority population, principally Latino, is paying the highest price. Workers cannot afford to live where they work or work where they live.

The political inability to direct state investment to address the urban infrastructure crisis in Texas is forcing local governments to confront spending limits, respond to emergency failures of critical infrastructure, and deny needed funding for the elderly, disabled, and chronically ill residents suffering under restrictive health insurance and health-care policies.

These examples of worst-case online stories are illustrative of decisions and events now actually occurring in regions that have failed to act while they could sustain the benefits of their prosperity in the long run. The question for state, regional, and urban leaders in the emerging megaregion is this: With so much data available and with predictive models of growth so reliable, will Austin and San Antonio and the corridor cities come together to address the region's growing pains while there is still time to do so? Will cities and counties working with the state meet the infrastructure challenges that will enable growth to be sustained and prosperity to expand?

"We are stronger as a region," said San Antonio business leader Graham Weston. "Together, we can punch above our weight. It's to our mutual advantage. Austin and San Antonio have a tradition as rivals. They've been like oil and water. We saw each other as different beings. But we're stronger together."

Industrial and economic planning by business leaders in each city can strengthen economic development throughout the metros, expanding the specialties of each city, focusing on education across the region, and making the case for needed infrastructure. The principal chambers of commerce in Austin, San Antonio, New Braunfels, and San Marcos can set up joint working committees or task forces to study and make recommendations to the governing bodies up and down the corridor. A summit between the Austin and San Antonio chambers of commerce was planned for the summer of 2023 as a step in that direction but was indefinitely postponed as multiple chambers sought new chief executives.

Regional cooperative planning could happen in several ways. More than thirty years ago, the Greater Austin–San Antonio Corridor Council was formed, with offices in San Marcos. It has focused principally on mobility issues. The corridor council's role should be expanded and strengthened with renewed urgency. The same could happen with the councils of governments in the two metros—the Alamo Area Council of Governments and the Capital Area Council of Governments—joining together for urgent studies and recommendations. The point of such multilevel regional collaboration would be to focus the requisite attention, action, and resources on the overarching and inevitable challenges before the region. Yet collaboration can be elusive.

A recent Brookings Institution report states,

Over the past decade, states are preempting local decision making more frequently and more harshly. Partisan culture wars are dominating state legislative sessions and prompting states to exert control over multiple policies that were once determined locally. Meanwhile, local employers and regional business groups are caught in the crosshairs, with some business leaders under assault for their efforts to advance economic inclusion and a tolerant workplace. When states strip power from localities, they can hurt community problem-solving and state-local coordination around matters of revitalization and opportunity ... state hostility toward cities can negatively impact joint approaches to economic prosperity and place-based opportunity—goals which states, local leaders, and multisector groups often share.

That same Brookings report notes that metro areas generate the majority of state economic output in forty-six of fifty states. In other words, metro areas provide revenues that support rural needs, including linking entrepreneurs in small towns to urban customers. This must be better understood in Texas' urban-rural economic blend.

A summary of the imperatives for regional action—a manifesto for action—would include the following.

Mobility

A prerequisite for a functional megaregion is effective mobility. That means acting upon the entire range of transportation options—roadways, arterial streets, advanced bus routes, rail systems, and trail- and bike-path interconnections. Failure to design an interconnected mobility system when the need is so obvious can only be termed *willful neglect*. Continuation of that neglect across the Austin–San Antonio region would run head-on into vastly increasing numbers of cars and trucks on the roads and people seeking public transit.

Austin voters have been the most responsive in approving a $10 billion package of mobility improvements, including an expansion of I-35, the connecting spine of the Austin–San Antonio region. San Antonio is expanding its freeway system and particularly its outer circumferential roadway, Loop 1604, as well as planning two intersecting routes of advanced rapid transit buses. Among the imperatives of the future are east-west connecting roadways to divert traffic from I-35 to the lesser-used SH 130 at the eastern edge of the region, short-term bus connections between Austin and San Antonio, and a light-rail route along I-35. Construction of arterial streets and connector roads must stay ahead of the new manufacturing plants and new residences that are rapidly building in job generators such as Lockhart, Seguin, San Marcos, New Braunfels, Boerne, Georgetown, Round Rock, Leander, and other cities growing at nationally significant rates.

Despite the planning failure of the 2003–16 Lone Star Rail District connecting Austin and San Antonio, a passenger rail across the corridor is not a dead idea. If Amtrak expansion is included in new federal infrastructure spending projects, the 240-mile Texas Central project connecting Houston and DFW, stalled because of public-domain court cases and rising cost estimates, could be revived as a public-private rail system, according to a 2023 *Washington Post* report. If that happens, the once promising Austin–San Antonio passenger train project also could be resurrected as a less costly and shorter two-city route with corridor stops, taking tens of thousands of vehicles off the interstate.

Water

North Texas leaders worked for many decades to acquire water supplies from as far north as the Red River to make possible extraordinary growth in the DFW metro area. As Central Texas becomes more arid and is subjected to extreme heat and prolonged droughts, it will be imperative to secure more groundwater sources, emphasize a deeper water conservation ethic, and apply new technologies to water solutions such as brackish sources, desalination, and advanced water reuse. All of Texas, especially the Austin–San Antonio region, should study water technology advances occurring in other states, such as direct potable water reuse. This technology, using reverse osmosis and ozone-combined-with-biofiltration processes, can make local wastewater reusable as drinking water, which could prove critical in times of prolonged drought, according to a *WaterWorld* newsletter. The same newsletter reports steps California is pursuing to protect groundwater in forty basins. The steps, aimed at preventing the overdrafting of groundwater basins, are coordinated through the California Department of Water Resources. California also is a leader in new technologies emerging for the desalination of sea and brackish water. Desalination presently is a costly and energy-intensive process, a problem that could be solved by harnessing green energy—wind and solar—as those renewable sources become more available and large-scale battery storage becomes more feasible, *WaterWorld* has reported. Storage is the key to "load balancing" water supplies.

Imagine, for example, a coastal Texas city being able to switch to stored desalinated water and then transfer some of its surface water reservoir supplies back to upriver basins for use by inland cities.

Arizona is stepping up in the water-storage arena due to recent restrictions on the state's ability to draw from the drought-stricken Colorado River basin. Phoenix has stored more than three trillion gallons, essentially a thirty-year supply. Housing developers in Arizona, for example, must prove to the state that a one-hundred-year water supply exists before commencing construction of new housing, according to *WaterWorld*. The number of options is rising nationally. The inadequacy of water supplies is the megaregion's most significant vulnerability, with the potential to stop the economic momentum.

Power

Blessed with large municipally owned power generation and distribution systems in much of the region, public-sector leaders have the authority to push for the growth of power reserves and to explain the need to the public. Both Austin and San Antonio are leaders in the use of renewable power generation and will continue to invest in wind and solar and, in the years ahead, hydrogen, carbon capture, thermal, and other emerging technologies. The future requires attention to power conservation, distributed power grid innovations, climate policies, and power-sharing arrangements.

The 2021 Inflation Reduction Act (IRA) aims to generate a significant boost in renewable energy production because of production tax credits and investment tax credits. Funding also will come for "green hydrogen" production that would compete with battery storage that makes green energy in general more reliable.

Rising summer temperatures and extreme polar vortexes in the winter threaten the state's vulnerable power grid. The state must implement improvements to the grid, including upgrades to generators and other equipment that can withstand extreme temperatures. Rising temperatures take their toll on streets and highways. The Associated Press reported in 2023 that US road maintenance costs could hit $26 billion by 2040 because of heat.

Pre-K-12 Education

The fastest-growing sector of investment in public facilities in the Austin–San Antonio megaregion is school facilities. That is because of the rapid increases in the school-age population, now surpassing 5.5 million students eighteen or younger, across the region resulting from the in-migration of younger families, the rate of new household formations, and the larger family sizes attributable to the growing Latino demographic. School districts in the region are pressed to add new classroom space at existing schools as well as to add entirely new schools. New elementary and middle schools create a need for new high schools. Several school districts in the region are among those with the fastest-growing student enrollments in the state. The Northside, North East, and San Antonio school districts from the San Antonio metro area are among the twenty-fifth-largest school districts in Texas, as are the Austin and Round Rock school districts from the Austin metro area. The Pflugerville, Georgetown, Hutto, Jarrell, Liberty Hill, Leander,

Comal, Boerne, and Medina Valley school districts—all within the Austin–San Antonio megaregion—are among the fastest growing in the state. Educational leaders must plan capital programs and operations budgets to match the growth. Careful attention to balanced state funding for public education is necessary to offset differences in property tax capabilities between valuation-rich and valuation-poor communities. To the degree that school expenditure imbalances perpetuate school performance gaps, the region's economic prospects will suffer. High-performance schools must be the goal across the entire region, even as Texas continues to invest less per capita dollars in public school students than most states.

Open Space Preservation

With strong pressures for land development across the region, it is necessary to set aside the open spaces, natural waterways, sensitive topographical features, and recharge areas now or they will be paved over and invisible to future generations. This is a subject area where failure to act today guarantees erasure from the landscape of major features of the attractive outdoor culture of the region. This is the time to use conservation easements, land purchases, and park designations to protect large swaths of open spaces, lakes, rivers, creeks, and springs. Projects such as the one-hundred-mile Great Springs linear park connecting Austin and San Antonio, the Mission Reach of the San Antonio River, the San Antonio Arboretum, and Austin's downtown Waterloo Park are critical to the balanced lifestyle of the region. All are reasons so many people want to live in the heart of Texas.

The Great Springs Project will take decades to complete. Its specific path depends on land availability and right-of-way concessions. Garry Merritt, Great Springs Project CEO, said no other similar greenway and springs system in the nation connects two large US cities like this one will. The San Antonio Arboretum is in the early stages of development and will be on the site of a South Side former golf course. Along the corridor, New Braunfels's Guadalupe River and Landa Park are legendary. San Marcos, home

> We need to have a development pattern that is healthier. That way we can conserve the kind of land and resources that are so beautiful throughout our cities. Otherwise, we would just be gobbled up. If our development pattern is just to pave everything, you are going to need more and more roads and cost more money. We have to develop right and make the investments smarter.
>
> —US Rep. Greg Casar

to the San Marcos River and San Marcos Springs, has invested in renovating its Rio Vista Park and the riverside walkway. Austin's natural beauty is highlighted by Zilker Park and the park's Barton Springs and pool, the Lady Bird Johnson Wildflower Center, Mount Bonnell with its lookout points, and the city's crown jewel, Lady Bird Lake. Formerly known as Town Lake, Lady Bird Lake's hiking and running trails give residents and visitors an oasis right downtown.

Environmental Responsibility

Rapid growth generates environmental concerns, some of which can be significantly deleterious to the quality of life. Beyond mere inconveniences, there are environmental effects that seriously impact human health. Air quality is damaged by toxic discharges, industrial pollution, ozone imbalances, vehicle emissions, extractive excavations, methane leaks, and levels of allergens. Water quality is diminished by human wastewater discharges, industrial processes, leaks from buried tanks, spillage from solid-waste treatment, and the overdrafting of underground reservoirs. Each of these challenges presently threatens air and water quality at specific points in the region. The overall environmental quality of the Austin–San Antonio region is markedly better than in many traditional industrial areas of the nation, but growth on the scale now occurring in the region and expected in the future requires responsible monitoring of the environmental effects.

Housing

In previous decades, housing prices in Central and South Texas were among the most reasonable in the nation. However, the combination of rapid population growth and insufficient housing production to keep pace with demand, particularly in the Austin area, has increased housing prices at double-digit annual rates. Median sales prices in Austin rose from $400,000 in 2021 to $605,000 in June 2023, an increase of 51 percent in two years. Average apartment rentals in Austin during that time rose from $1,450/month to $1,806/month, an increase of 24.5 percent. Local governments have proposed policy changes to facilitate more production of all types of housing by changing zoning regulations, reducing minimum lot sizes, expediting permits, reducing parking requirements, and lowering fees. The goals must be to build more affordable housing, preserve the existing housing stock, prevent displacement of lower-income residents, and create permanent housing for homeless persons. Executing these policies will in great measure determine whether the Austin–San Antonio megaregion can sustain affordable housing for the young professionals who are essential to the companies and firms that are the cornerstones of the region's economic future.

Air Connectivity

In the years following World War II, as air travel was extended to a broader cross section of travelers, American cities tended to regard their airports as useful conveniences for their residents. Over the last decades of the twentieth century, however, the basic narrative about cities and airports flipped. John Kasarda wrote in his book *Aerotropolis* that the connectivity of direct air routes has become the fundamental differentiator between those cities that will be the recognized engines of the American economy and cities that will assume lesser positions in the urban hierarchy. The hub-and-spoke system that the airlines devised has firmly cemented a hierarchy. Neither Austin nor San Antonio is an airline hub. In that sense, their air connectivity has been in the shadow of DFW International Airport, with its hubs for American Airlines at DFW Airport and for Southwest Airlines at Love Field, and of Houston, with its hub for United Airlines at Bush International Airport. For decades, both Austin and San Antonio have sought additional nonstop flights to other large cities to prevent residents from enduring time-consuming plane changes in Dallas or Houston. While both cities have added more nonstop flights, Austin has distanced itself with significantly more business travelers generated by Austin's tech sector and individuals with more disposable income for national and international leisure travel. San Antonio is investing heavily in its central-city airport, adding new terminals and passenger conveniences. Concepts for a massive regional airport have been considered and dismissed, appropriately, considering the distances from the northern suburbs of Austin and the southern side of San Antonio to any mid-point site. In the long run, the region will join the ranks of metropolitan areas that manage multiple airports through some measure of cooperation. Without hub status, the impetus will have to be the sheer weight of regional economic success and traveler demand that makes the case for more direct routes from each airport. If the Austin–San Antonio region is going to benefit from Kasarda's concept of air connectivity as the decisive driver of economic momentum, regional leaders will have to continually promote direct air connections conveniently accessed from both airports with all the modern amenities found in hub airports.

Higher Education

An estimated 300,000 students attend higher education institutions in the Austin–San Antonio region. That is a massive amount of human capital acquiring new skills, and waves of talented graduates seek opportunities across the region. The region's higher education assets include several very large public institutions such as the University of Texas at Austin with 53,082 students in 2023, its campus in San Antonio at the University of Texas at San Antonio with 34,864 students, Texas State University in San Marcos with 38,873 students, and Texas A&M University–San Antonio with 7,619 students. The region is blessed to have high-quality small private colleges such as Southwestern University in Georgetown, Texas Lutheran College in Seguin, and Trinity University in San Antonio, among others. It has a cluster of Catholic universities of higher education, including Our Lady of the Lake, St. Mary's University, University of the Incarnate Word in San Antonio, and St. Edward's University in Austin. There are a host of other institutions of higher education in the region, including the Alamo Colleges with five campuses and 66,000 students, which effectively cover the southern half of the region, and Austin Community College with eleven campuses and more than 70,000 students in the northern reaches of the megaregion.

Recognizing the rigorous education demands of the new economy with its computer technology and biosciences concentrations, it is imperative that the region's competitive higher education institutions be sustained and enhanced. Public leaders and business advocates throughout the region have understandably strong motivations to support the expansion of both degree programs and cutting-edge research. That will not happen without greater funding for public higher education in the state budget for every form of assistance to students through loans, grants, work-study programs, and supporting collaborative projects with businesses.

Social Cohesion

As in many metropolitan areas in the nation, the evolving demographics of the Austin–San Antonio region are transforming. The most obvious of those demographic changes are related to ethnic identification and national origin. The Latino community in the region is growing at dramatically faster rates than the non-Latino population. The reasons are rooted in the history of the region, its proximity to the US-Mexico border, the larger size of Latino families, and in-migration. Comparisons of current population percentages for the core counties of the region for just the most recent twenty years for which data are available make the point (see tables 12.1 and 12.2).

Table 12.1.

Bexar County (San Antonio) ethnic population percentages

Ethnicity	2000	2010	2020	2050 (projected)
Latino	54.4%	58.7%	59.3%	61.2%
Anglo	35.6%	30.3%	25.9%	19.6%
African American	6.9%	6.9%	6.9%	8.2%
Asian	1.5%	2.3%	2.3%	7.3%

Table 12.2.

Travis County (Austin) ethnic population percentages

Ethnicity	2000	2010	2020	2050 (projected)
Latino	28.2%	33.5%	34.8%	39.5%
Anglo	56.4%	50.5%	47.7%	39.8%
African American	9.3%	8.1%	8.2%	8.4%
Asian	4.5%	5.7%	6.7%	8.3%

Sources: Texas Demographic Center, US Census Bureau, and author calculations.

Note: The percentages are rounded and do not add up to 100 percent. The remainder is categorized as "other."

From these comparisons, it is evident that Latinos will continue to increase as a percentage of the area's total population over the next three decades, more than any other ethnicity numerically. Anglos are projected to drop in percentages through 2050, while African Americans and Asians will see rising percentages. These numbers are significant because the populations—Anglo, African American, and Asian—differ measurably with respect to income gaps, educational disparities, and wealth measures. They participate in the workforce differently and therefore have differences in wage levels, buying power, savings rates, homeownership roles, college attendance, selection of neighborhoods, and other critical determinants of quality of life. Segregation by neighborhood, school district, and even social groupings are visible aspects of life in the region. These separations in turn affect political outlooks and social mobility. Educational attainment, experts in all fields agree, is the surest path out of poverty and into the economic mainstream and the promise of living healthier, more prosperous lives.

The comparisons of key indicators from selected places across the region underscore the significance of demographic trends (see tables 12.3, 12.4, and 12.5).

Table 12.3.

Poverty levels by race in San Antonio and Austin

Race	San Antonio	Austin
Anglo	14.2%	9.7%
Black	23.1%	23.1%
Latino	19.7%	21.1%
Asian	11.1%	7.5%

Source: US Census Bureau American Community Survey, 2021 estimates data.

Table 12.4.

Median income by race in San Antonio and Austin

Race	San Antonio	Austin
Anglo	$63,539	$88,576
Black	$41,751	$48,350
Latino	$50,337	$57,894
Asian	$82,776	$111,480

Source: US Census Bureau American Community Survey, 2021 estimates data.

Table 12.5.

Educational attainment of a bachelor's degree for people aged twenty-five and older by race in San Antonio and Austin

Race	San Antonio	Austin
Anglo	47.3%	67.8%
Black	24.0%	37.0%
Latino	19.1%	35.8%
Asian	57.0%	77.0%

Source: US Census Bureau American Community Survey, 2021 estimates data.

188 • Chapter 12

These social indicators make it clear that Black and Latino poverty rates are significantly higher than Anglo poverty rates in both San Antonio and Austin. Almost a quarter of African Americans in both Austin and San Antonio—precisely equal at 23.1 percent—live in poverty. In both cities, about one-fifth of Latinos live in poverty.

The disparities are a reflection of the substantially lower median income levels for Black and Latino residents in both cities. African Americans in San Antonio have the lowest median incomes in either city; African Americans in Austin have the widest gap in median incomes, more than $40,000 below the Anglo median income and more than $63,000 below the Asian median income in Austin. Gaps of these dimensions in incomes invariably result in wide divergence in family wealth, housing opportunities, school options, and general quality of life.

The Asian communities in both cities have the highest incomes and the lowest poverty rates, attributable to the steady influx of Asian professionals to the region.

It is also notable from these comparisons that all ethnic groups across the board have higher incomes in Austin than in San Antonio. However, Latinos have slightly higher poverty rates in Austin than Latinos in San Antonio. It is also evident that the disparate poverty rates and incomes across ethnic groups in the region correlate with great disparities in educational attainment measured by the percentage of people aged twenty-five and older who have attained a bachelor's degree. Austin percentages for all groups are on average a significant 18 percent higher than San Antonio's. But the gaps between Anglo and Asian average levels of educational attainment and Latino and African American average levels in both cities are stunning—average gaps are more than 30 percentage points in San Antonio and 36 percentage points in Austin. Educational gaps of this magnitude go far to explain the income and poverty disparities in the region, but they are even more troubling for the future. When the fastest-growing demographic groups in the region are already far behind in incomes and when educational gaps promise to perpetuate or even worsen those disparities, dangerous social challenges lie ahead. Put another way, when the fastest-growing demographic groups for the future have the lowest educational statistics stretching into the future, those lagging groups can never expect their incomes to catch up.

Racial and national origin distributions should not alone be factors in projecting the economic future of the region. However, if those distributions become synonymous with the continuation of vast disparities in educational opportunities, wage and wealth levels, and housing opportunities in perpetuity, then the social cohesion of the region will be severely tested. For example, it becomes politically more difficult to generate the needed across-the-board support for bond issues for transit solutions, new schools, or basic infrastructure if there exists a perception among growing populations that the benefits are not spread equitably. It must be made clear by policy decisions and actions that the benefits of growth—jobs, incomes, wealth, and opportunities—will fuel a steadily improving quality of life for all ethnic, racial, and income groups.

Social Needs

In every metropolitan area in the nation, even the most prosperous, there is a segment of the population with urgent needs for human services. There are segments of the American population broadly who are disabled, low-income elderly, unhoused, or in other ways marginalized from the mainstream economy. The Austin–San Antonio region is no exception. It is a given that in this region, those populations will remain heavily reliant on local government support as well as charitable and philanthropic efforts. The social net of nonprofits serving these populations, however, is susceptible to economic downturns, which affect giving and threaten organizational viability. Serving the outlying communities where social resources are far scarcer poses another challenge. Simply stated, the scale of the problems requires more than episodic solutions and more continuous forms of social care.

In Texas, unequal access to health care for millions of adults and children has a direct negative impact on life expectancy, access to preventative health care and prenatal care, the rate of infant mortality, the quality of advanced senior care, and the burden on public and private hospitals and clinics where the uninsured often frequent emergency rooms for otherwise unavoidable medical attention to ailments minor and major. The state of Texas' failure to participate in the federal Medicaid insurance program results in high percentages of uninsured individuals and families and therefore limited access to doctors, clinics, and preventative care. Fortunately, Austin and San Antonio are positive examples of metropolitan areas that have taken steps proactively to forge local responses. The creation of the Dell Medical School in Austin was a joint effort with the University of Texas and Seton Hospital and had as a goal to improve health-care access for lower-income residents. In San Antonio, Bexar County's University Hospital is beginning a program of construction for three regional hospitals to improve medical access across the county. These are permanent, continuous, and broad-based solutions to the Texas-specific problem of the medically uninsured.

Even in our nation's most vaunted economic engines—San Francisco, Boston, Minneapolis, and New York—America's city leaders have yet to devise the economic frameworks and services delivery system that can cover all residents in need. Everywhere across the nation, 10 to 20 percent of the urban population is deprived of an uplifting quality of life. Austin–San Antonio leaders, working with proven, dedicated nonprofit providers—those working selflessly in the fields of homelessness, disabilities, foster care, mental health, hunger and nutrition, veteran's assistance, addictions, aging, and other needs—should include alongside their economic objectives a goal to create a regional exemplar of compassionate and competent human services.

Funding Needs

The challenges created by the steady growth of the Austin–San Antonio region generate a need for reliable and continuous funding. So much infrastructure must be built from the ground up—schools, power stations, water pipelines, roadways, mass transit, open spaces, airport improvements, college and university buildings, housing, and human services facilities—that new sources of revenues must be identified. It will be necessary to deploy local resources, federal dollars, state assistance, and new approaches to acquiring private capital. Those investments will pay off in returns from taxes and fees to be assessed upon new and expanding businesses and residential communities.

Both Austin and San Antonio have recognized that need in recent years and devised creative ways to generate local funding. In 2020, Austin voters approved a $10 billion package of mobility-related expansions that included new light-rail routes, dedicated bus lanes, and massive renovations, including the tunneling of gridlocked I-35, which transverses the center of the city. The revenue streams combined sales taxes and property taxes dedicated exclusively to transportation investments. The level of public frustration with highway traffic congestion, overcrowded arterials, and travel delays was so acute that, as unacceptable as tax increases generally are, voters overwhelmingly passed an unprecedented series of revenue propositions.

Also in 2020, voters in San Antonio approved a complex package of measures to fund the extension of a successful municipal pre-kindergarten program, authorized a new advanced skills-training fund, and dedicated a permanent funding stream for mass transit. To make some of this funding possible, the city administration identified a new mechanism to fund purchases of development rights over the recharge zone of the Edwards Aquifer, which is the city's principal water supply. By voting for extensions of sales taxes, San Antonio voters in one action prioritized education and skills training to meet the challenges of the new economy and generated revenues for advanced rapid transit bus lines, all with the understanding that protection of the city's water supply was funded. These are examples of the kinds of actions that the public in the Austin–San Antonio regions will have to consider in the years ahead to fund the full extent of essential infrastructure.

Another major source of capital that regional governments will use is federal funding, both grants and loans, from such measures as the Infrastructure Investment and Jobs Act (IIJA), the Inflation Reduction Act, and the CHIPS semiconductor legislation. The IIJA and the IRA total more than $1.25 trillion in federal spending, according to the Brookings Institution. All are already being deployed to fund regional transportation, airport, water, workforce training, education, and open space projects. Building and maintaining the region's infrastructure with federal dollars will be essential to ensuring the region's increasing contributions to the nation's economy, competitiveness, and national security.

The role of the state budget will also become more significant as it is clear that the state's economy is ever more dependent on its urban areas. The state of Texas already is a major funder of public education, higher education, water development, and highways—all of which are vital to local cities and regions. Despite its legendary rural history, Texas today is one of the most urban states in the nation, with twenty-five metropolitan areas. The divisive state politics of recent years that pits growing cities against rural areas and suburban populations on matters such as annexation, policing, and local revenue sources, and often enough sees cities and the state facing off in courtrooms, has great potential to damage these important engines of the modern Texas economy. Overly restrictive state laws can damage not only local governments but also state revenues. The principal bases of revenues of future state budgets will be the industries, businesses, and households in Texas' urban areas. To feed that revenue machine going forward, it will be essential to expand the state's funding role in areas such as prekindergarten education, workforce training, mass transit, and urban parks.

Private capital from across the nation and across the world is increasingly being invested in the Austin–San Antonio megaregion. Most of that private capital will be deployed into profit-generating industries and commercial businesses, yet some will be deployed into public-private partnerships to fund infrastructure improvements to ports, airports, highways, and mass transit. The financial world is well aware of growth in the Austin–San Antonio region, characterized as among the most attractive investment opportunities to be found anywhere.

The Austin and San Antonio metros must keep an eye on remaining competitive in the US urban landscape. In 2022, the Harvard Business School's Young American Leaders Program issued a report focusing on economic metrics in eighteen US cities, including Austin and San Antonio, as measured over a fifteen-year period from 2005 to 2020. The survey demonstrates that the two cities are surprisingly similar in some measures, while different in other ways. Both were leaders in compound annual population growth: Austin ranked second at 2.9 percent annually, while San Antonio was fourth at 2.1 percent. That alone makes this region the growth leader; none of the other sixteen cities are in close proximity to one another.

Austin and San Antonio are two of the three youngest cities in median age. Austin's median age is 35, while San Antonio's is 34.9, a similarity that sends a powerful message of future economic, job, and population growth. Expanding business enterprises go where the growing workforce is found. So it's no surprise that another similarity is the compound annual growth of private-sector jobs between 2001 and 2020. Austin led the nation at 3.3 percent yearly. San Antonio, historically a big military and government city, was number two at 2.2 percent.

The Austin and San Antonio metros are more homogenous in income inequality, too, despite widely held views that associate Latino poverty with San Antonio and far greater prosperity in Austin. Both metros ranked among the best cities in the nation in the degree of inequality. The same is true for upward mobility, the capacity for low-income residents to rise to the middle and upper classes through education and opportunities. San Antonio ranked number eight, and Austin number nine. Austin and San Antonio both rank poorly in K-12 public spending per student, as of 2019. Austin ranked thirteenth among US cities, and San Antonio sixteenth, reflecting the state's record for inadequate public school funding. Both cities also ranked poorly in the percentages of people without health insurance in 2020. San Antonio led the nation with 15.2 percent of its residents uninsured. Austin was fourth at 12.1 percent.

Austin and San Antonio also rank at or near the bottom of the surveyed cities for voter turnouts and participation in US Census

Bureau surveys. San Antonio was the worst in the nation, and Austin ranked thirteen out of sixteen. This could be attributed to voter suppression efforts in Texas as well as "don't care, doesn't matter" attitudes.

By other measures, the cities are different. Median household income in 2022 was $86,556 in Austin and 25 percent lower at $59,593 in San Antonio. Compound annual growth in median household income was 3.2 percent in Austin and 2.4 percent in San Antonio between 2005 and 2020. Accordingly, Austin's poverty rate is lower, at 12.4 percent, versus San Antonio's 17.7 percent in 2022. The income disparities are not unrelated to education outcomes. Austin's high school graduation rate was 91.1 percent in 2020; San Antonio's was 83.8 percent. More than 56 percent of adults in Austin have a four-year degree versus 27 percent in San Antonio. In Austin, 17 percent of adults have a graduate degree versus 11 percent in San Antonio.

The picture that emerges from the Harvard study is that Austin is more prosperous than San Antonio, and it is attracting more in-migration and thus growing faster, as projected by the Texas Demographic Center. Cooperation and better planning across the thirteen counties could narrow the gap, improving the quality of life among all residents in the corridor.

* * *

As noted in the opening chapter, our initial motivation to write this book was our astonishment at the most recent US Census numbers reporting population growth rates across the Austin–San Antonio region, including in the many corridor cities and those outside the corridor in the two metro areas, and even more so by the projections of growth for the next several decades. Our assumption was that few residents of the area have reflected on the significance of living in a megaregion of five million people that will add more than three million more by 2050, the same period of time that has elapsed since 1996. Our impulse was to explore the numbers and their implications and explain how they usher Austin–San Antonio into the major leagues of national and even global urban centers.

It became clear, however, that we would not be doing much of a service to readers by simply reporting the numbers. We felt obligated to examine the implications. That led to a second purpose for writing the book: to review not only the opportunities such growth offers but also the challenges of preparing for and sustaining that growth.

The upsides are significant: better jobs, higher incomes, wider opportunities, resources for quality-of-life amenities, and stronger prospects to achieve excellence for institutions from universities and public schools to medical centers and leading-edge businesses. That trajectory from the present to the future has a precondition: Basic support systems of the region must keep pace, and wherever they already are inadequate to meet current needs, major initiatives must be undertaken to meet future needs. Many growth regions across the nation have stumbled on the assumption that somehow growth and its attendant needs will all take care of itself. Instead, other megaregions have found that "the goose that lays the golden eggs requires care, attention, and resources as well as bold, visionary leadership." We decided to look more deeply into the dynamics of how the region will change and what is required to prepare for that change. Thirdly, we have labored here to identify the priority areas that leadership must address with commitment and urgency. The book is a call to action to prepare now for unprecedented growth that can make this entire region one of the most dynamic, prosperous, and unified regions of the nation. Understanding where other cities and regions have failed is essential to avoid such an outcome here. We know the most significant challenges that are in plain sight for all to see. We recommend deliberation with purpose and action with forethought. The central conclusion of this book is not that the actions we identify are essential for the region to grow. The region is going to grow no matter what we do. The Austin–San Antonio megaregion is an economic hot spot and people magnet. There are many well-understood reasons: unlimited land to grow, a ready workforce, cutting-edge industry, a younger demographic profile, favorable state tax frameworks, unfavorable business conditions in other states, and the many legends of the mythic Texas spirit. We are going to grow whether we want to or not!

All of us want to live in and raise our families in a region with the highest possible quality of life, the greatest economic mobility, the most uplifting communities, and the most promising prospects for happy lives for everyone who lives here. That can and will happen if we get to work now.

APPENDIX 1

Selected Austin–San Antonio Metro Cities and Percent Population Growth, 2010–2023

City	2010 population	2023 population	Percent change
Austin	790,407	979,882	23.97%
Bastrop	7,218	11,679	61.80%
Boerne	10,471	21,774	107.95%
Buda	7,295	16,030	119.74%
Cedar Park	48,937	77,516	58.40%
Dripping Springs	1,788	8,689	385.96%
Floresville	6,448	8,306	28.82%
Georgetown	47,400	96,312	103.19%
Kyle	28,016	62,548	123.26%
Lockhart	12,698	15,318	20.63%
New Braunfels	57,740	110,958	92.17%
Pflugerville	46,936	65,301	39.13%
Round Rock	99,887	130,406	30.55%
San Antonio	1,237,407	1,495,295	12.65%
San Marcos	44,894	71,569	59.42%
Schertz	31,465	43,239	37.42%
Seguin	25,175	36,013	43.05%
Universal City	18,530	20,028	8.08%

Source: US Census Bureau and author calculations.

Note: The percentages are rounded.

Population Growth Projections for Austin–San Antonio Metro Counties, 2023–2060

Austin metro county	2023	2050	2060
Travis	1,334,961	2,035,923	2,252,137
Williamson	697,191	1,360,139	1,682,556
Hays	280,486	721,388	1,003,130
Bastrop	110,778	184,520	223,711
Caldwell	49,859	69,133	76,291
Austin metro counties total	**2,473,275**	4,371,103	5,237,825
San Antonio metro county	**2023**	**2050**	**2060**
Bexar	2,087,679	2,865,834	3,102,720
Comal	193,928	434,242	584,380
Guadalupe	188,454	326,154	387,211
Medina	54,797	60,148	61,719
Wilson	54,183	67,968	73,304
Atascosa	51,537	61,473	64,960
Kendall	50,537	89,665	111,448
Bandera	22,637	22,139	22,586
SA metro counties total	**2,703,752**	3,927,623	4,408,328
Austin–San Antonio metros total	**5,177,027**	**8,298,726**	**9,646,153**

Source: Texas Demographic Center.

Note: The numbers assume the continuation of the 2010–20 population growth rates.

INDEX

Note: Page numbers in italics refer to figures and tables.